ISBN 978-1-331-58005-8
PIBN 10208488

1 MONTH OF
FREE
READING

at

www.ForgottenBooks.com

By purchasing this book you are eligible for one month membership to ForgottenBooks.com, giving you unlimited access to our entire collection of over 700,000 titles via our web site and mobile apps.

To claim your free month visit:
www.forgottenbooks.com/free208488

Similar Books Are Available from
www.forgottenbooks.com

THE YOUNG KING AND QUEEN "FELL ON THEIR KNEES, AND ASKED GOD
TO HELP THEM."

STORIES

OF THE

FRENCH REVOLUTION

EDITED BY

WALTER MONTGOMERY

FULLY ILLUSTRATED

BOSTON

ESTES AND LAURIAT

PUBLISHERS

University Press:
JOHN WILSON AND SON, CAMBRIDGE, U.S.A.

CONTENTS.

—————oo⚇oo—————

LIST OF ILLUSTRATIONS.

8 LIST OF ILLUSTRATIONS.

STORIES OF THE FRENCH REVOLUTION.

Stories of the French Revolution.

CHAPTER I.

THE OLD KING DIES.

ABOUT eight miles from Paris is the town of Versailles, which was but a poor little village when a great king took a fancy to it and built there a palace. His son was passionately fond of state and grandeur, and he resolved to add to the palace, room after room and gallery after gallery, until he had made it the most superb house in all the world. It is said the cost was so frightful that he never let any one know what the sum total amounted to, but threw the accounts into the fire. This was Louis XIV., called by Frenchmen "Le grand Monarque." He reigned seventy-two years, having been a mere child ·when called to the throne.

To this splendid palace and to an income of thirty millions a year, did his great-grandson, Louis XV., succeed. He, too, was a child of tender years when he entered on his vast inheritance. For a time the Duke of Orleans acted as regent; but when the little king was fourteen years of age he assumed the sceptre, and in two years more he married a Polish princess.

· At one time Louis was very much beloved, and got the title of "Bien Aimé;" but he afterward lost his people's affection, and by the time he died he was utterly despised, if not detested. Everything seemed to be going to rack and ruin. The French armies were defeated, their colonies fell into the hands of England, their navy suffered great losses, their commerce was all but ruined. Therefore the French people felt disgraced; and many of them believed all these evils were greatly owing to the idleness and bad management of their pleasure-loving and careless king.

At length, one year, — it was in the pleasant May-time, — Louis fell sick of small-pox. He was at once put to bed, and the doctors came to see him; but from the first they looked with grave anxiety on the ailing man. His three daughters — whom he had nicknamed Rag, Snip, and Pig — waited on him dutifully, though the terrible disease turned everybody sick who came near the bed. The stench was carried far into the palace; but there the princesses remained until the end came. They had a fourth sister, nicknamed Dud; but she was in a nunnery, and so could not wait upon her dying father.

So Louis, once the " Well Beloved," lay dying at last. Twice before he had been near death. Once at Metz he was very, very ill, and prayers ascended in every church for his recovery; and at another time he almost perished under the knife of an assassin, named Damiens, who leaped on the carriage-step and stabbed the king in the side. But now Death had come to him in earnest, and Louis was nevermore to smell the roses in the glorious gardens of Versailles, nor was he evermore to watch the wonderful fountains play, nor to hunt in the pleasant forest. Death had called for him at last, and he must go. When he felt himself sinking into the grave, he sent for the sacrament, and it was given him by Cardinal Roche Aymon. Many ministers of religion were praying incessantly in the chapel below for the king's recovery. While the dauphin (afterward Louis XVI.), his queen, and many of the courtiers were present at one of these services, the May skies were darkened by a sudden thunder-storm, and the rattling peals drowned the sound of the chants and prayers. The tempest rolled away, and soon after the old king breathed his last.

While he was in his death agonies, the dauphin and his wife and others were standing ready to leave Versailles at a moment's notice. The horses were yoked to the carriages, and the postilions in their churn-boots were standing by; all were ready for an instant start. At length the dauphin and Marie Antoinette heard a noise like the sound of distant thunder; it came nearer and nearer, and very soon the door of the apartment flew open, and all the courtiers crowded in, each wishing to outstrip the other in saluting the new majesties of France.

The young couple, it is said, fell on their knees and asked God to help them to rule, for they were so young and knew not how. It was a pious deed; and we cannot but grieve as we see them, full of youth and hope and prosperity, beginning that course which so soon afterward ended in disaster and death.

It seems strange to us that Louis did not remain at Versailles and follow his grandfather to the grave. Wicked as he was, the old king might at least have had a decent funeral. As for the young king, he and his brilliant court did not remain an hour, but stepped into their carriages and were driven away at a rapid rate to Choisy. Meanwhile the dishonored body of the late monarch, now a mass of putrefying sores, was tumbled hastily into a coffin of lead, which was well supplied with spirits of wine. The coffin was then carried rapidly away by torchlight to St. Denis, where the kings of France had a burial-place. As the funeral procession passed through Paris, many were the bitter things said of him who was gone. The curious people stood in two rows to witness the dismal sight pass them at a quick trot.

Ten years of peace followed the accession of Louis XVI.; but he and his government had been meanwhile getting deeper and deeper into debt and discredit, and they were at length obliged, by sheer want of money, to call together a parliament, called the States-General, which had not met for upward of a hundred and fifty years.

CHAPTER II.

THE poor people in France were in a most miserable condition. Bread was very dear, and grievance of many kinds abounded. Once, not long after the young king ascended the throne, the poor rose up, and went with a petition to Versailles. The king appeared on a balcony, and spoke to them not unkindly; but by the advice of his ministers, two of the leaders were hanged on a new gallows.

The king by and by had to reduce the expenses of his household, and Versailles became an altered place. The wolf-hounds were given up; then the bear-hounds; then the falcons; and one nobleman after another, who had a good salary, was dismissed.

A minister named Calonne, a clever man, did some service for a while in raising money, and so making the king's path easier; but it was all moonshine, as we say. Things were really getting worse. Calonne then proposed to do a very wise thing, we think; namely, to call together the notables, — a thing which had not been done as long as the king could rule without them. These notables were peers, dignified churchmen, soldiers, lawyers, and men of mark, to the number of one hundred and thirty-seven, who sat in seven companies, each under a prince. Calonne was for taxing *all*, — even the upper classes, who stupidly thought they ought to be free. This was so little liked that Calonne had to resign and leave the country in haste.

After nine weeks' chatter the notables departed each to his home, without having done much, except to pave the way for a National Assembly.

A clever Swiss banker, named Necker, had also labored, like Calonne, in the thorny path of managing the king's money-bags; but as he, like Calonne, advised that the Clergy and Nobles should be taxed, he was dismissed, but called back again amid the plaudits of the people. Necker's portrait was carried aloft in a procession through the streets of Paris; while a wicker figure of an archbishop who was very unpopular was burned on the Pont Neuf by a wild mob. A charge of cavalry was made, and many people killed and wounded.

No States-General had met for one hundred and seventy-four years, and it was a hard matter to know how to get them to work together. But it was at last decided they should meet, to get France out of her troubles; and so the king sent a signal through the land in the frosty January of 1789. Men were everywhere ordered to elect their members, and to draw up a list of their grievances. And of grievances there was no end. In the month of April the members elected were arriving at Versailles, hunting up lodgings, and making preparations for the opening day. But before that day arrived, a terrible event had taken place in Paris, showing the violence of the people. A certain paper-manufacturer, named Reveillon, had his works in the most unruly part of Paris, named St. Antoine. Reveillon had been heard to say that a journeyman paper-maker might live well on fifteen sous a day. This seems to have roused the wrath of the rough inhabitants of St. Antoine, and they gathered with menacing looks about the manufactory. Reveillon sent for some soldiers, who cleared the street, and posted themselves therein for the night.

But on the morrow matters grew worse, and so another detachment of troops was ordered to the spot. These men could hardly with gun and bayonet reach it, so choked with lumber and crowds was the street. The soldiers fired at the mob, who were already in the building engaged on the work of destruction, and the mob replied with yells and showers of stones and tiles. As the riot went on, some of the king's Swiss Guards, with two pieces of cannon, were sent; and whén the rioters saw the steady, determined faces of the redcoats and their lighted matches, they slank away into their dens, leaving no less than four or five hundred dead men in that one street. The unfortunate paper-maker, who had lost all but his life, took refuge in the Bastille, and the dead were buried with the title of " Defenders of their Country."

Twelve hundred and fourteen gentlemen were now assembled at Versailles, and each one kissed the king's hand in the palace. It was noticed, however, that while the Nobles and Clergy had *both* folding-doors thrown open for them, the members of the third estate, or Commons, had only *one* opened for them. A spacious hall had been prepared, the king taking great interest in its fitting up. There was room in it for six hundred Commoners in front, for three hundred Clergy on one side, and three hundred Nobles on the other.

On Monday, May 4, the town of Versailles was a human sea. Mèn clustered thick about roofs and chimneys, and every window was thronged with sight-seers, all intent on the march of the twelve hundred deputies from the Church of St. Louis, where they assembled, to the Church of Our Lady, where they were to hear a sermon. The Commons walked in black ; the Nobles in embroidered velvet and plumes ; the Clergy in their proper robes. After them came the king and queen and royal household. Several men afterward famous were among the Commons ; as Danton, Camille, Desmoulins, and Mirabeau. There, too, went the bilious Robespierre, spectacles on nose ; and there was Dr. Guillotin, who gave his name to the instrument of death. " With my machine," said he, " I whisk off your head in a moment, and you feel no pain." One clergyman, the Abbé Sièyes, sat among the Commons.

Next day the States-General assembled in their noble hall, and the king made a speech to them. When he finished, he put on his hat. The Nobles followed suit, and put on their hats ; and then the third estate, or Commons, did the same. Then arose a cry, " Hats off !

SOLDIERS FIRING ON THE MOB.

Hats off!" And some cried, "Hats on!" The king, to put an end to a ridiculous dispute, took his own hat off again. This was but a slight thing, but it showed the temper of the Commons.

For six whole weeks the Commons did nothing but wait. They saw the Nobles and Clergy wanted to sit and act separately, and they were resolved to do nothing at all, until they could all act together as one body in one chamber, This the king and court did all they could to prevent, fearing lest the weight of the Commons should incline the whole States-General to take the direction of liberty, equality, and fraternity, — things which the privileged classes always have hated and always will.

CHAPTER III.

THE TENNIS-COURT OATH.

THE Commons, you remember, would not do anything at all, because the Clergy and Nobles refused to sit and debate with them. The king and his council did not wish the Clergy and Nobles to sit and talk with the Commons, for they were afraid the Commons would make them too liberal; and they were the more afraid because one hundred and forty-nine out of the six hundred Clergy joined the Commons. These were mostly clergy of the lower orders, and what we call parish priests. This made the court resolve to do something. Some were for planting cannon opposite the hall of debate, so as to terrify the Commons into obedience. Others were for shutting up the hall and turning them into the street. The king was always a mild man and against doing anything violently, and he did not approve of the cannon business at all. He was therefore persuaded to order the Marquis de Brezé to shut the doors of the hall.

On Saturday, June 20, therefore, when the hour of meeting came, the President of the Commons, whose name was Bailly, went, in company with the members, to the hall. Bailly had received a letter from the marquis, which told him that the Commons would not be allowed to use the hall; but this letter Bailly put in his pocket and did not notice. When he and the Commons reached the door, they found it guarded by soldiers, and within carpenters were at work, making the hall ready for some grand court ceremonial. The captain of the guard politely informed Bailly that he could not let the members in, and he showed the king's order. They might send some of their number in, to remove any papers that might belong to them, but nothing more. So Bailly and his secretaries went in, and carried off the papers, with minds full of anger. The members stood some minutes under the shade of a fine avenue of trees, considering what was best to be done. They felt sure that the courtiers were chuckling over their disappointment. The morning was cloudy, and a drizzling rain began to fall. Great was the hubbub of voices under the friendly shelter of the trees; loud were the complaints and cries of shame; many the plans of what to do next. Some were for meeting in a large courtyard called the Place of Arms; others were for going over to Marly, whither it was heard the king had driven; some were for forcing an entrance into Versailles Palace itself. But it was soon rumored that President Bailly had found a convenient place. It was a tennis-court in the street of St. Francis, and thither the disgusted Commons took their way. It was a bare place, enclosed by four naked walls. A table and chair were borrowed of a neighbor, and, the President and his friends having opened their papers, the proceedings began with a solemn oath! A certain Monsieur Mailly proposed that the six hundred members should lift up their right hands to Heaven, and swear they would meet anywhere and under any and every circumstance, until they had made suitable laws for the right government of France. When the oath was sworn, each member took a pen and signed his name. There was only one man who refused, — a member from Languedoc; and him they declared to be "wrong in his head."

When the members had agreed to meet on the Monday following in the Récollets Church, they separated. Bailly had shown himself a worthy leader, and was at that hour the most popular man in France; but the court party were dreadfully vexed. When Monday came, myriads of people flocked into Versailles to see what might turn up. The king, perhaps alarmed, put off his ceremonial; and the Commons, in a solid body, marched to the church, where they found the one hundred and forty-nine Clergy awaiting them. There was a scene of much emotion, men embracing each other and shedding tears. The next day (a very rainy day) the king invited the States-General to enter the hall, where he made a speech. He declared his resolve that the three orders should vote separately. A number of articles were then read aloud, and the king said if they could not agree upon them he would effect them himself. " Let each order," said he, " now depart, to meet to-morrow in its own place, to despatch business." Then all filed out, except the Commons and those Clergy who had joined them.

It was now that Mirabeau showed himself as a leader of men. He rose to speak. While on his legs the Marquis de Brezé interfered with, " Messieurs, you have heard the king's orders ! "

" Yes," replied Mirabeau, " we have all heard what the king has been advised to say, but you are not the man to remind us of it. Go, sir, and tell those who sent you that we are here by the will of the people, and nothing but the force of bayonets shall drive us hence ! "

It was not thought prudent to send soldiers to expel the audacious Commons; for they seemed inclined to show a mutinous spirit. A ruse was therefore tried. A *posse* of carpenters was sent into the hall to remove, with much hammering and noise, the platform. It was hoped their clatter would drown the orators, and stop the proceedings. But, lo ! the carpenters, when they had worked a few minutes, stood open-mouthed on the platform, listening with wonder to the finest speaker they had ever heard. Mirabeau was now moving that the Commons were a National Assembly, and that any person who dared lay a finger on any member should be guilty of a capital crime. This was put to the meeting, and made a decree. Before the week was out the rest of the Clergy and the Nobles had joined the Commons, the king begging them to oblige him by yielding to what was clearly the popular will. It was the last day of June when the States-General

THE TENNIS-COURT OATH.

were united in one house; and great was the joy and many the lighted torches carried about everywhere.

But though the king had yielded to the Commons, he had done it very unwillingly; and he still hoped to punish his rebellious subjects by means of the sword, if he could do it in no other way. Suspicion of his purpose was aroused by the marching of regiments and the rumbling of great guns. Cannon were pointed at the Assembly Hall, and the members were alarmed by the tramp of armed men and the never-ceasing tap of the drumstick on the drum. The general, named Broglie, had his headquarters in Versailles, and all the day long aides-de-camp were coming and going. Something was up, without a doubt, and some terrible damage would certainly have been done to the rebellious part of the States-General if it had not been for one fortunate thing, which was this, — the soldiers positively refused to draw trigger when their muskets were to be pointed at their brother Frenchmen! They made a solemn promise to each other in the ranks that they would never act against the National Assembly. In fact, the privates in the French army, having nothing to lose and all to gain, were as eager for change as the citizens, and quite ready to disobey their lordly officers if the orders given did not please them.

CHAPTER IV.

THE FALL OF THE BASTILLE.

A PICTURE of the Bastille, or State-prison, shows us a great mass of masonry, with round towers. It stood at the east end of Paris, in the street of St. Antoine. It was begun in 1369, and finished in 1383. Its strong walls were surrounded by a wide ditch, which itself was defended on its outer side by a wall thirty-six feet high. The towers had several eight-sided rooms one over another, each with a narrow window. There was no fireplace, and no article of furniture, except an iron grating raised six inches from the floor, and on this the prisoner's bed was laid. The rooms in the walls were more comfortable. The interior consisted of two courts, called the "Great Court" and the "Court of the Well." The prison had a well-paid governor, several officers poorly paid, and a certain number of Invalides and Swiss, who had a small daily allowance, with firewood and candles. One unhappy prisoner was confined in these dreary walls for fifty-four years. Two prisoners, and only two, ever managed to escape. They contrived to make two ladders, which they hid under the floor; and one dark night they climbed up the chimney, cut through the iron gratings, and got on the roof. Thence they descended about one hundred feet to the bottom of the fosse or ditch. Then they made a hole in the wall next the Rue St. Antoine, and so escaped. This was Feb. 26, 1756.

The month of July, 1789, had come. It was now Sunday, the 12th, and, owing to all those movements of troops we spoke of toward Paris and Versailles, the minds of all were in a flutter. Great placards on the walls urged you to keep indoors; but if you did not, you could hardly move without meeting a foreign soldier. " We are to be mown down, then, are we ? " asked one citizen of another. Had you been in Paris that Sunday, you might have seen Camille Desmoulins — poet, editor, and speaker — mount a table with a pistol in each hand, and ask the crowd around " whether they were willing to die like hunted hares. The hour is come," cried Camille, "and now it is either death or deliverance forever. To arms ! " A thousand voices echoed the last words of Camille, " To arms ! " He then said, " My friends, we must have some sign to know each other by ; let us wear cockades of green : green is the color of hope ! " The multitude then rushed to embrace Camille; and some one handed him a piece of green ribbon, which he pinned in his hat. Next, they went to an image shop, where they got two wax busts, — one of the favorite minister Necker, who had been just dismissed, and the other of the Duke of Orleans, a royal prince who hated the king, and became for a time on that account one of the leaders of the revolution. The multitude now kept moving on and growing in numbers. Armed with all sorts of weapons, they soon came into collision with the foreign troops, who, by order of Prince Lambesc; fired on them, and hacked at them with their sabres. The mob dispersed, but only to reunite in some other place. " To arms ! To arms ! " resounded all over Paris. The bells were tolled at sunset ; the shops of gunsmiths were broken open and rifled ; the blood of the great city rose to boiling heat that evening. Around the Hôtel de Ville a raging multitude clamored for arms all night; but the authorities knew not what to do, and slipped away as best they could. A few daring spirits took their places, and sat up all night at the Hôtel, giving such directions as they thought best, and ordered a Paris militia to be at once enrolled.

Monday morning broke on the restless city. There was no work done in Paris that day, except by the smiths who were making pikes, and by the women who were sewing at cockades. These were not green, however, but red, white, and blue. All shops but those of the bakers and wine-sellers were closed. " Arms! Arms! Give us arms!" — such were the constant cries. About three hundred and sixty fire-locks belonging to the old city watch were served out. The Arsenal was broken open, but nothing was found inside except rubbish. Two small Siamese cannon and some swords and armor were snatched from the king's armory. Deserters from the regular army came trooping in. At two in the afternoon more than three thousand good soldiers left their officers and joined the mob. The newly ordered militia of Paris already numbered many tens of thousands, but arms were yet few. Fifty thousand pikes, however, were made in thirty-six hours; so the smiths were busy enough.

It oozed out that in the cellars of the Invalides Hôtel there were twenty-eight thousand muskets. The governor there was an old man named Sombreuil, whom we shall hear of again. He, suspecting his old soldiers of siding too much with the rioters, ordered them to unscrew the muskets; but they went to work very unwillingly, and in six hours had done very little. About nine o'clock on Tuesday morning the Invalides Hôtel was attacked and broken into, and the arms found, amid great rejoicing; and now, having got so many useful arms, the cry was raised, "To the Bastille! To the Bastille!"

The governor's name was De Launay. He had eighty-two old Invalides in the Bastille, and thirty-two Swiss. His walls were nine feet thick, and he had cannon and powder; but he had only one day's supply of food. About noon a man named Thuriot obtained admit-tance into the prison. He found De Launay unwilling to surrender, — nay, he threatened to blow the prison into the air. Thuriot and De Launay went on the battlements, and the governor turned quite pale at the sight of Paris rolling onward against the doomed Bastille. But he would not yield; he would die rather. A second and third deputation tried to move the governor; but his patience waxing thin, he pulled up the drawbridge and ordered his men to fire on the people.

THE FALL OF THE BASTILLE.

And now began a dreadful scene. Men fell wounded or dying here and there; shouts rose incessantly, mingled with ceaseless volleys of musketry. An old soldier, named Louis Tournay, was seen striking with his axe at the outer chain of the drawbridge: he was aided by another veteran, named Bonnemère; and at length the chain was broken, and the ponderous drawbridge fell thundering down into the ditch.

Two officers chanced to be in Paris at the time, named Elie and Hulin. These men directed the troops, while a marine, just come from Brest, levelled the Siamese cannon against the walls. Men who were wounded were carried away, and those who were dying entreated the assailants not to cease fighting until the cursed prison was level with the ground. Three fresh deputations arrived from the Hôtel de Ville, asking De Launay to surrender, and promising him favorable terms; he, however, could not hear what was said, owing to the great noise, or, if he guessed what they said, did not believe them. And so the furious fight went on, from one o'clock, when it began, until five, when the Invalides made a white flag, and a port-hole was opened, as if some one would hold a parley. A man named Maillard advanced gingerly on a plank toward the port-hole, snatched a letter held out to him by a Swiss, and returned. It ran thus: "The Bastille shall be surrendered, if pardon is granted to all." The promise was given on the word of one of the officers, and the second drawbridge was lowered, and the mob rushed in. The Swiss stood grouped together in their white frocks; and there too were the Invalides, all disarmed. The first comers, who had heard the bargain, meant to be true to their word; but they could not, — for others, mad with vengeance, came up, and in a few moments one of the Swiss soldiers who tried to escape was killed, and an Invalide lost his right hand. The rest were marched off to the Town-hall to be tried for the crime of slaying citizens. De Launay, dressed in a gray frock with a poppy-colored ribbon, was about to stab himself, when some people interfered and bore him off, escorted by Hulin and Maillard, to the Hôtel de Ville. On the way, however, the miserable De Launay was torn from the shelter of his escort, and brutally murdered. The only part of him that reached the Town-hall was "his bloody hair *queue* held up in a bloody hand." One or two others of the garrison were massacred; the rest were saved, though with much difficulty, by the Gardes Françaises. Inside the hotel Elie was busy forming a list of the Bastille heroes. Outside was a perfect forest of spears and bayonets. Along the streets were carried the seven prisoners found in the Bastille, also seven heads on pikes, also the keys of the captured fortress. Through the whole of the following night the stones of which the prison had been built came down with a sound of thunder.

And what of the king's palace? That very evening there was a grand ball in the Orangery. It was "Nero fiddling while Rome was burning," once more. In the dead of night the Duke of Liancourt came to the king's bedside and told him what the Paris mob had done.

"Why, it is a revolt!" said Louis.

"It is more," replied the duke: "it is a revolution!"

CHAPTER V

THE BURNING OF THE CHÂTEAUX.

LONG had the French laboring-classes been trodden down by the French Nobles. We have not the faintest idea now of the miserable bondage in which the poor people were held before the days of the Great Revolution. The fall of the Bastille seems to have aroused them like a clap of thunder. They rubbed their eyes as men awakened from a deep sleep, and asked whether it were real, or whether they were like those who dream. The wretched down-trodden slaves rose up with the bitter recollection in their hearts of ages of ill-usage, and with a keen relish for vengeance. Amply did they revenge themselves on the seigneurs, as the lords were called. These men generally idled their lives away in their elegant country-mansions or in the gay circles of Paris. They drew their means of enjoyment from rack-rented estates and from grievous dues; and their tenants were ground down with penury and misery.

One day, it is said, Louis XV., when hunting gayly as his custom was, met a ragged peasant with a coffin at the corner of some green alley in the wood of Senart. He stopped the man and asked him who was going to be buried in the coffin, and the man told him.

" What did he die of?" inquired the king.

" Of hunger," replied the peasant.

It is to be feared that was a very common disease in those evil days. Every now and then this bitter hunger drove the people to rebellion; and in 1775 they gathered in great crowds, as we have already heard, around the palace of Versailles, clamoring for bread.

The king showed himself on the balcony, and spoke soothing words to them ; but two of their number were hanged on a new gallows forty feet in height, and that was the answer they got, — an answer not soon forgotten.

The old Marquis Mirabeau, in his Memoirs, has drawn a painful picture of the French peasantry. He describes them as "savages descending from the mountains," as "frightful men, or rather, frightful wild animals, . . . their faces haggard, and covered with long greasy hair; the upper part of the face pale, the lower part distorting itself into the attempt at a cruel laugh. You can fancy you may starve these people with impunity," said he, "always till the catastrophe comes. Such government as this will end in the general overturn." And it did come when those "haggard wretches," as the marquis called them, rose up against their superiors and drove them from their homes.

Soon after the fall of the Bastille many of the highest in the land, afraid of losing their lives, hastily left the country, and some of them had much difficulty in escaping. Prince Condé was pursued to the Oise; and others fled in disguise, with friends in lieu of servants on their coach-boxes

One immensely rich man named Foulon (whom the people hated with a deadly hatred because he had said they might eat grass) thought to escape them by pretending to be dead and buried; but about a week after the fall of the Bastille he was found alive, and one morning early the villagers of Vitry, where he lived, dragged him to Paris. Bareheaded and decked with nettles and thistles, he was hurried to the Hôtel de Ville to be judged. After some time a man stepped forward and said, "What is the use of judging this man ? Has he not been judged these thirty years ? "

The yelling crowd applauded, and the old man was put to death without further loss of time. He was hanged to a lamp-iron, pleading for life, but in vain; and after he was dead his body was dragged

BERTHIER SEIZED BY THE PARIS MOB.

through the streets, and his head was carried about on a pike-point, the mouth filled with grass.

His son-in-law named Berthier was also arrested and brought from Compiègne to Paris. He was a brave man, but his look became ashy when he met Foulon's head on a pike-point. Though Berthier was protected by a large body of men with drawn swords, the mob broke through them and snatched him out of his escort's hands. He seized hold of a musket and defended himself with the courage of a lion, but it was all in vain. He was hanged on the same lamp-iron, and his head and his heart also flew over Paris.

These two may serve as instances of the hatred of the people toward their rich oppressors. " These men were the tyrants of the poor," said their murderers; "they drank the blood of the widow and of the orphan."

A great stillness had fallen on Versailles. How. different it was now from what it had been a year or two ago! The queen had become the most hated woman in France, and often shed many tears; and the king must have felt his throne tottering beneath him. It was a fearful hour. Bread was dear, and grew dearer day by day. Money was very scarce, and the people's hearts were heavy and bitter. An Englishman named Arthur Young has left a book behind him in which he tells of many things he saw in his travels through distracted France. He once overtook a poor woman who, though not yet twenty-eight, looked at least sixty years old. She told how hardly they had to live, she and her husband and seven children, and how poor they were after paying rents and quitrents, hens to one lord and sacks of oats to another. Besides these, and taxes to the king and other dues, the good man was obliged to do a certain amount of statute labor, for which he got no pay. It was no wonder that the poor woman said, " The dues and taxes crush us."

And now, when the Bastille had fallen and the people had found out their strength, the work of destruction went on all over France.

Every night the darkness was dispelled by some great fire. The church bell of the village was rung, and the whole parish assembled to commit havoc as they chose. And they often chose to wreak their vengeance on the church itself; for the clergy, as being a privileged class, were almost as much hated as the great lords.

These great lords, with their delicate ladies and children, were obliged to fly, often by night, glad enough to escape with their lives. The tax-gatherers had to disappear, their occupation gone at least for a season.

The same Arthur Young says: " The grand seigneurs were shocking bad landlords. They lived in the midst of ill-managed fields and wastes, and great woods filled with deer, wild boars, and wolves. If I were King of France for one day," said he, " I would make these great lords skip again!"

They did not combine, as they perhaps might have done, in their own defence; but they were scattered widely over France, and were often jealous of each other, though no one doubts their courage. One man did indeed rid the earth of a number of his poorer neighbors by inviting them to a banquet at his château, and then killing them by igniting a barrel of gunpowder.

Of course law was not yet utterly powerless to put down robbery and mob violence. Some of the house-burning ruffians were tried, condemned, and hanged on trees by the roadside as a terror to evil-doers.

Such, then, were the scenes common in France in the summer months of 1789. The wheels of industry ceased turning; the soldiers seemed disposed to be mutinous; and at Strasburg they openly embraced the mob, and helped them set fire to the Town-hall.

It was hardly safe, as Arthur Young found, to travel about France in those evil days. Many times shot and slugs came whistling about his ears, and sometimes his carriage was hit by them. Whether he was aimed at as an aristocrat flying the country, or whether the badly aiming peasants "shot at the pigeon and hit the crow," we are not told; but he complains of the thing in his book. During this autumn the "first emigration," as it is called, went on without ceasing; and many landed on the shores of England.

Meanwhile hunger pressed heavily on the people, who had to stand m long *queues*, or tails, at the bakers' shops. This was done so that they who came first were first served, and the others in the order of their coming. A man would sometimes stand half a day in a queue, and then receive only a bit of dear bad bread. A rigid search was made all over the country for grain; and farmers who would not sell, and bakers who adulterated their bread, were threatened with the halter. The bread at St. Denis was so bad and black that the people hanged the mayor for it. The corn-market at Paris had to be guarded by six hundred soldiers. Thus went on the French Revolution in the summer and autumn of 1789.

CHAPTER VI.

THE FATAL BANQUET.

TOWARD the end of September, 1789, the suspicions of the people of Paris became yet more aroused. The question was hotly debated, whether the king was or was not to have the power to " veto " — that is, to forbid — any particular law to be enacted. A certain violent speaker, named Huruge, who went to petition against the king's having this power, was thrown into prison; and General Lafayette and his soldiers had to be very strict in dispersing crowds and putting street-speakers to silence. Several newspaper printers and editors were seized, one of them being the well-known Marat, who was the most advanced republican, and who issued a paper called " The Friend of the People." These things did not please the multitude; and moreover the scarcity of bread seemed to increase, and it was observed that the boat which brought grain from Corbeil paid only one visit to Paris instead of two every day. It was maddening to the mothers, who had children crying for bread in vain, to hear of grand dinners being given at Versailles. This was an aggravation of their own miserable state, and it led to what will be hereafter described as the Insurrection of Women. The grand dinners which went on at Versailles we will now attempt to describe.

On the 23d of September, then, a dashing regiment, called that of Flanders, marched into the town of Versailles, trailing after them two pieces of cannon. Marat, before he was put in prison, went over to Versailles, and there saw evident signs of the king's doubling his guards and introducing foreign troops for the purpose of putting down

THE FATAL BANQUET.

the people by force. When the regiment of Flanders had settled itself in the barracks at Versailles, the Royal Body Guards thought it would be only right to invite the new-comers to a dinner; and the date fixed for the repast was Thursday, the 1st of October. But where were they to find a room large enough to dine in? Among the stately buildings which made up the immense palace there was one very seldom used, — the Opera House; and it occurred to some ingenious man that this would be the very place for the grand banquet.

The king readily granted the request, and in the Opera House the feast was held. Now it happened that after the dinner was done, various toasts were drunk; and while the merriment was at its height the low-spirited queen was persuaded to enter the Opera House and look down on the brilliant scene. She therefore did so, with her little son in her arms and her husband by her side.

There was a loud outburst of loyal feeling as the royal family walked round the dinner-tables; and by design or chance the band struck up a tune which went to the words " O Richard! O my king, the whole world is forsaking thee!"

The guests at once saw the fitness of the music to the circumstances of the king, and they became greatly excited. They drew their swords and waved them about; they tore off their tricolor cockades, trampled them under their feet, and replaced them by white ones (the old Bourbon color).

This dinner was followed by other dinners on the 2d and 3d of October, when the white cockade was worn by all. These favors were made of a large size, as if to show a greater loyalty to the king and his family. Some wore black cockades, as if they were mourning for the king in his troubles; and several had the courage to appear with them in the streets of Paris. The people felt insulted by these black badges; and one national soldier at the Tuileries parade on Sunday morning, the 4th of October, started from the ranks, and wrenched a black cockade from some one who was wearing it, and trod it angrily in the dirt. Another man who wore a black cockade had it torn off; and when he attempted to replace it, a hundred sticks started up around him, and he was obliged to leave it where it was. Another nearly fell a victim to the lamp-iron, being saved from the rage of the people by the National Guards and General Lafayette.

That same Sunday, the 4th of October, was a very disturbed day in Paris. Tidings of the banquets at Versailles were now being talkèd about all over the city, and thousands of hungry people were saying, "We are starving; but yonder, at the king's palace, there is plenty and to spare."

For the first time in the French Revolution there was seen, on the evening before, a woman engaged in public speaking. "My husband's tongue has been put to silence," said she, "but I will speak;" and speak she did to a great crowd all the thoughts which filled her heaving bosom, and made it ready to break.

A new idea seemed to strike the women of Paris that same night, and it was nursed all the next day. It was this, — to have a rising of their own. If General Lafayette and his men had silenced and put down their husbands, they would never be such dastards as to pierce women's hearts with their bayonets, would they? This was the thought uppermost in the hearts of the women of Paris — that is, the poor women with hungry children — during that October Sunday in the year 1789. And, as we shall see, the thought became a deed, when, on the Monday following, tens of thousands of women, with an earnest purpose in their minds, marched on the palace of Versailles.

CHAPTER VII.

THE INSURRECTION OF WOMEN.

ON Monday morning, the 5th of October, Paris awoke to face once more a day of bitter want. Mothers heard their children crying for the bread which they could not give them; and when they sallied forth to see what could be got, they met others on the same dreary errand.

One young woman seized a drum and beat it, crying out at the same time to all mothers to assemble and go somewhere. A vast mob soon flocked to the sound of her drum; and they bent their steps first of all toward the Town-hall, or Hôtel de Ville, which they reached about seven o'clock. The patrol were greatly surprised to see eight or ten thousand women mount the outer stairs, and the foremost levelled their bayonets to keep them back, but this was found impossible. The soldiers had to open their ranks and let the women through. They then hurried up the stairs, along the passages, and through the rooms. The major-general, Gouvion, was in the building; but what to do he knew not. He chanced to have a cunning man with him, named Maillard; and Maillard stole out by a secret staircase, and caught hold of another drum, which he beat furiously outside. He thus drew off the women, who were doing much mischief. Angry at not finding the mayor, or any one to help them, they seized Abbé Lefevre in the belfry and nearly hanged him; they splintered doors with axes, took away guns, and even cannon and bags of money, and were on the point of setting the fine old place on fire.

When Maillard's drum was heard outside, the women streamed forth, and shouts of " To Versailles! to Versailles!" rent the air. Cart-horses were made to draw the cannon; and on they all went to the Champs Elysées, where they halted. Maillard here persuaded them to nominate officers, and then to march with some kind of order, and with as few arms as possible, to present their request for bread to the king and Assembly at Versailles. The day was miserable; and on the sloppy road walked many a lady in her shoes of silk, — not because she liked it, but because she was compelled.

The news flew before the mob, and Mirabeau whispered to the President: " Paris is marching upon us. Go over to the Château and tell them." As soon as the women were well on the road, Gouvion collected a large force of National Guards. These men had felt the insult offered in the dinner business, and they sent to their general, Lafayette, to say that they would never turn their bayonets on the women, but they would go and abolish that insolent regiment of Flanders, and those Body Guards who had trampled on the tricolor cockade. They would then bring the king to Paris, where he ought to live. The general was amazed, and argued half the day against it; then he tried to escape, but his men would not let him go, and there he sat on his white charger for hours, while the soldiers and people kept shouting " To Versailles!" At length the general gave way, and about three o'clock moved thither with thirty thousand men; a vast mob, irregularly armed, going on in front.

Maillard and his women halted on a rise above Versailles, and he pointed out the place where the Assembly was then debating. " Now," said he, " let us put these arms out of sight, and all appearance of sorrow, and let us sing." And so the women advanced up the dripping elm avenue, singing " Henri Quatre." The king, who had gone shooting, was hastily fetched back, and the soldiers were dispersed about the palace in a posture of defence. While Mirabeau and the others were debating, in came Maillard and fifteen draggled women.

. THE INSURRECTION OF WOMEN.

He had had to use all his powers to keep the others outside. He spoke, and then the women cried out, " Bread ! bread ! " It was agreed that the president should take some of the women to the palace, and he went out with them. But others crowded round him, begging to be taken also ; and he was obliged to add twelve more. As they went they were scattered by some insolent horse soldiers who rode among their ranks, and it was only with much difficulty that they managed to reach the gate.

Five of them were allowed to see the king ; and one of these, a maker of figures, and a handsome girl, nearly fainted ; whereupon the king supported her in his arms. When they went again into the crowd, this same young woman was nearly strangled by the others, who were angry at the notice taken of her by Louis. " She has no children that want bread," cried they ; " only alabaster dolls which cannot eat." Poor Louison was in peril of death. The garter was round her neck, and strong arms pulling at each end, when she was rescued by two soldiers.

It was a most miserable afternoon, and the soldiers were wet, and losing patience, and slashing at people every now and then with their swords. One had his arm broken by a stray bullet, and the horse of another was killed ; of course these things did not mend matters. The cannon which had been trailed all the way from the Hôtel de Ville were now levelled at the palace gate, but the powder was too damp to ignite. At length the Body Guards were ordered to retire, as their presence was irritating to the mob ; and whenever one showed himself at door or window, he was cursed and fired at. Then a rumor flew about that the king had got his coach ready as if for flight, and a sharp look-out was kept on the back gates.

There was a certain draper, named Lecointre, who was rather famous in these times of trouble. He now rode off to ask the mayor for six hundred loaves, but he could not get them nor aught else at present ; so they skinned and roasted the dead war-horse, and ate its flesh with much relish. 4

When the president got back, he found his Assembly-hall filled with women, making speeches and passing resolutions. A stout woman was comfortably seated in his own chair. Before she would give it up she told him they were all very hungry and must have something to eat. He took the hint, and sent round for food, which came at last, — bread, sausages, and some wine. The members now edged their way in, and began to discuss the Penal Code. One of the women said, " What is the use of the Penal Code? What we want is bread ! "

About the middle of that strange night Lafayette and his Nationals arrived, having spent nine hours on the road. Before reaching Versailles he had made his men swear to respect the king's house. He was admitted to an audience, and told Louis he must do four things for the sake of peace, — he must be guarded by the National Guards ; he must get bread for the people ; he must have all the prisoners in Paris tried, and, if found innocent, set free ; and lastly, he must come and live in Paris. The king granted the first three readily, the last not so readily.

Toward three in the morning, the sentries having been set, and other business done, sleep fell on the distracted multitudes ; and after two more hours of consultation with his officers, Lafayette flung himself on his bed, tired out.

In the early dawn a Body Guard, looking out of a window in the palace, saw some prowling fellows below. Ill words were spoken ; and the soldier, waxing wroth, fired off his piece. Others returned it, and after some shots a young man in the crowd received his death-blow. Then there arose a fearful shriek from the mob, and a rush at the outer gate, which swept it open. The inner gate was also battered in, and then the people rushed up the grand staircase into the palace. Two sentries were trodden down and murdered, and the rest had to retire into a room and barricade the door, which was soon shivered to pieces.

The savage mob went raging on toward the queen's suite of rooms, in the farthest of which she was now sleeping. Some sentries before-hand with the crowd knocked, and cried, "Save the queen!" Two officers of the Body Guard showed vast courage at that terrible hour, and by their heroic efforts stemmed the flood until the queen was able to get into the king's bedchamber. One of these men, Mismandre, was left for dead at the outside of the queen's door, but he was able to crawl away and join his comrades.

From the king's bedroom they could hear afar off the noise of axes and hammers thundering on the doors. The rage of the people was directed mainly against the Body Guards, who were now driven into a large hall, and who heaped all sorts of things against the door. It shook under the blows dealt on it; but at the very moment it was giv-ing way the blows ceased suddenly, and a voice from the other side told that a body of friends were there. By this time, also, Lafayette and his Nationals were on the scene, and the mob were soon driven out of the palace to rage in the courts below. The two Body Guards who had been killed on the staircase were beheaded, and their heads carried on long pikes through the streets and away to Paris.

"The king to Paris!" — such was the cry now everywhere. "The king must come to Paris!" Nothing else would do. So at one o'clock the king agreed to start to Paris. When Lafayette announced the king's consent, there was a shout and a discharge of fire-arms. It was the knell of the glory of Versailles.

Cartloads of bread arrived from Paris, enough for all; and great was the joy of those who munched it. More than that, fifty wagon-loads of corn were found in Versailles, and carried in triumph to the famish-ing city.

The king was now the prisoner of the mob, and most men saw what a grave thing it was. He had been conquered, and the people had once more learned their own strength. Many people now left France, and sixty thousand emigrated to Switzerland alone.

One o'clock arrived, and the royal family entered their carriages;

but they did not start for another hour, — so long did it take to arrange the motley procession. What a sight it was! Men carrying loaves on pike-points, or guns with green boughs sticking out of the barrels. Some rode on cannons; and others, trying to mount the king's horses, were thrown, much to the amusement of the fickle mob.

"We shall not lack bread now," said some witty Parisian, "for we are bringing with us the baker, the baker's wife, and the baker's boy."

At the Town-hall the king was made to step on a balcony by torch-light. He wore an immense tricolor cockade in his hat. It was not until eleven o'clock on Tuesday night that he reached the Tuileries, sad enough no doubt. This was the sixth day of October, 1789.

CHAPTER VIII.

HAPPIER days followed the king's removal to Paris than were expected. The onward progress of the Revolution seemed for a time arrested. The palace of the Tuileries was splendidly furnished for the royal family, and the blue uniforms of the National Guards were ever seen patrolling before it. The little prince had a garden of his own, and a little summer-house, and tools to work with, and he might be watched at his work by the people as they passed along the street. The National Assembly held its sittings in the Riding School close by, and were constantly engaged in the work of a new Constitution.

The king no doubt felt the restraint laid upon him. He was free to go where he liked in the vast pile of the Tuileries and its spacious grounds; he was also free to be driven anywhere about Paris, where he was well received; but he was not free to roam the woods on a hunting expedition. He once more took to his favourite pursuit of lock-making, and, as we shall see, fitted up a secret iron safe in one of the walls, in which afterward many important State papers were found, some of which did him great damage at his trial. For forty-one months did Louis inhabit the palace, while the Revolution went on, sometimes slowly, sometimes rapidly, to its end.

Many of the senators, Mirabeau among them, saw that the power of the king was likely to be made too small, and they therefore tried to retain for him a certain part of the rule his ancestors had. On this account these men fell in the esteem of the masses. There were many of a different mind in the Assembly, — men like Robespierre and his party, who were for putting away the king altogether.

Beside the senators, who actually made the laws, there were two things which wielded great power. One was the newspapers; the other was the clubs. There were some papers loud for the king, others as loud for the people and dead against king and Nobles. Of those which were published against the king and Nobles, none was more bitter and outspoken than that edited by Marat, and called the "People's Friend." Among the clubs there was one which has become more famous than any club which ever was or ever will be. It was called the Jacobin Club. It got that name from its meeting in what was once the Church of the Jacobins. This club, which began among the Bretons, was always noted for its extreme violence. The most advanced Republicans belonged to it. The old church was seated for twelve hundred, and there was a gallery as well for women. There the leading spirits of the Revolution used to speak their burning words. No one was admitted there except by a ticket. At first the Jacobin Club was not hot enough for some, while it was too violent for others; and so two branches broke from it. Danton, of whom we shall hear much, formed the Club of the Cordeliers, which for a time was even hotter than that of the Jacobins; but he and those who followed him after a time returned to the Jacobin Club, which was called the Mother Society.

It happened one day that Louis thought it might do some good if he paid a visit to the National Assembly in the Riding School; so he sent word over to say he was coming. Some preparations were made for his visit, such as a purple covering with gold fleur-de-lis on it spread over the president's chair, so as to make it an impromptu throne, and a carpet laid down for his Majesty's feet. When Louis entered they all rose; and when he said a few simple words in his own simple way, they one and all gave him some hearty cheers. And when he was in his palace once more, some of the members were sent across to thank him for his kindness in visiting them ; and one of the senators proposed that they should all renew the National Oath.

This idea was acted on at once. Every member stood up and swore afresh to be true to king, law, and country ; and the oath was also renewed at the Town-hall, and in all the streets of Paris, where vast excited crowds swore under the canopy of heaven, while drums rolled and the city was illuminated. This was the fourth day of February, 1790.

And then the idea went forth from Paris into every corner of France. For three weeks the swearing of the oath went on, till it is supposed every French man and woman had taken it. One mother in Brittany gathered her ten children, and made them all take the oath in her presence ; so that in many cases the children swore as well as the parents.

But this simple visit of the king to the Assembly, and the simple act of one member suggesting that all the rest should renew the National Oath, led to a surprising scene in the following July ; for it occurred to some one that it would be a grand thing to assemble deputies from each department, or county or shire as we should say, in Paris, who there, as representing the whole of France, should swear the oath in the presence of the king, the army, the Assembly, and as many citizens as could be packed together.

Each town and city had its own swearing-day before the grand one at Paris. We read the account of a very fine one at Lyons, written by Madame Roland, the wife of the famous minister of state, — where there was a rock made of painted wood, fifty feet in height, with a huge figure of Liberty on the top and a sort of temple beneath. Fifty thousand men assembled on that occasion to swear, and there were four times that number of people looking on.

But as Paris was the greatest city of all, and the mother city, so her grand swearing-day was to surpass all others. It was decided that it should be on the same day as the fall of the Bastille and in the Champ de Mars, and nothing should be spared to make it the grandest thing of its kind. A huge sort of theatre was to be scooped out of the earth in the Champ de Mars by the spades of fifteen thousand workmen. But the work was not begun soon enough, and it seemed that the fifteen thousand were rather lazy, and refused to do more work when offered more wages; therefore, when they threw down their tools one July afternoon, a number of volunteers picked them up, and began to work with a will. The next day, instead of waiting till the spades and barrows were not in use, the excited citizens brought picks and shovels of their own, and came marching to the scene of action headed by young women carrying green boughs, and shouting the famous *Ça ira !* — "It shall go on!"

The effect was wonderful; you might count, if you cared to take the trouble, volunteer workers to the number of a hundred and fifty thousand, men of every trade and profession, — printers in paper caps, water-carriers, charcoal-men, the rag-sorter, and the elegant dandy, the lawyer and the judge, the mayor himself, and General Lafayette. The king came to see the strange sight, and was very well received. A number of men surrounded him, spades on shoulders, as a sort of body-guard suited to the occasion. He used afterward to say, poor man! that those days were some of the happiest he ever spent.

Even ladies came to help, and some patriotic wine-merchant would now and then trundle into the diggings a barrel of wine. So earnest were the laborers that no one thought of drinking any of the wine, except such as were faint from their unusual exertions. And so by means of all this genuine labor, so heartily bestowed, the huge space of three hundred thousand square feet was excavated, and so arranged that there were rows of grassy seats one above another to the number of thirty, all well rammed down and covered with turf.

In the centre, so as to be seen by all, there was a pyramid, called the Altar of the Country. Here the oath was to be sworn, — by

THE NATIONAL OATH : THE EXCAVATIONS.

General Lafayette for the army, by the king, and by deputies who came from every department in France.

When the great day arrived, it was a cold morning for July, and it looked as if rain might fall; but the people streamed in, and took their places where they would. Each of the eighty-three departments had sent a splendid banner; and a fine show the men made as they filed in and took their appointed stations. Lafayette took the oath first. He ascended the pyramid, pressed his sword-point on the altar, and pronounced the oath in the name of the whole army. The National Assembly swore where they stood, under the canopy; then the king swore, and there arose a shout, and citizen shook hands with citizen; and there was a clashing of arms, and a booming of great guns, which were listened for, and responded to as soon as heard, — so that all over France that afternoon the tidings of the oath at Paris was carried by one volley after another.

Perhaps it was this firing of cannon which brought down the long-impending shower. Anyhow the shower did come, and the seats were suddenly a canopy of umbrellas, and the flags drooped, and the ladies' dresses were spoiled. At three o'clock the sun shone out again, and the clouds went their way. A whole week was spent in brilliant feasts and merry-making. On the Sunday after the great oath-day a universal dance took place. The Elysian Fields were almost as bright as day with innumerable lamps, and filled with dancers all the livelong night; and where the grim old Bastille once reared its frowning walls one could read *Ici l'on danse*, beneath the tree of Liberty, sixty feet high, and topped with a cap of Liberty.

In fact, for a whole week or more Paris was almost wild with joy, and it was hoped, though the hope proved vain, that the Ship of State, after a few rough squalls, was now in calm waters, which were not again to be ruffled by serious storms.

CHAPTER IX.

TROÚBLES IN THE ARMY.

A T Metz, which is a strong fortress, an officer named Bouillè commanded the troops. He was an exceedingly brave man and a very loyal one. He looked upon the great National Oath with much dislike and suspicion. He did not approve of soldiers and citizens being too familiar with each other. He did not like his soldiers to mix freely with the people and imbibe their liberal ideas. He knew very well that the army was tainted with those notions, and the troops were becoming every day more mutinous. In those days no man could be an officer unless he was able to prove his nobility for at least *four* generations. The officers, therefore, were of the most select class, every man an aristocrat; and they spared no pains to show their dislike to these new and strange events. The privates were leavened with the popular spirit; they were beginning to think that one man is as good as another; they were beginning to resent the haughtiness of their officers; and they talked often and much over their own grievances.

One great grievance was that they were not paid their wages; and they believed the officers robbed them of their money. General Bouillè, therefore, at this time did not rest upon a bed of roses. He felt like a man who lives over a powder-magazine, where people go in and out with lighted matches. But his heart was like a rock; braver man than Bouillè never drew a sword. When the Regiment of Picardy boisterously embraced National Guards, and sang, and swore oaths together in disorderly array, the general had the men up in the barrack square, and gave them a bit of his mind very sharply. And when the Regiment of Salm advanced to the colonel's house to lay violent hands on the money-chest, Bouillè, hearing of it, ran before them, and stood like an iron statue on the outer stairs, sword in hand, keeping the whole regiment at bay. For two hours he stood there, supported by a few of his brother officers. Several times some wrathful soldier was persuaded by a hater of aristocrats to level his musket at the intrepid general; but in every case the barrel was struck aside before he could fire. Bouillè never flinched, nor cared a straw for aught any man among them might choose to do. After two hours the mayor interfered, and got the men back to their quarters by promises of pay, which were fulfilled in a measure the next day, when each soldier received half his arrears in cash.

So bad was the discipline of the army, indeed, that Mirabeau moved that it should be broken up and organized afresh; but his motion was not carried. The place where the army was in the worst possible position for drifting suddenly into open mutiny was Nanci in Lorraine. Nanci was more aristocratic than other places, both in her citizens and governors; but she had also a large population who were kept up to revolution pitch by a Jacobin Club; and there were here three fine regiments much tainted with the spreading evil, and quite ripe for mischief, — one especially so, that of Château Vieux. The officers at Nanci had made many objections to the oath-swearing which had gone on. At first they would not go at all to the Nanci meeting, and when they repented and went, they appeared in undress suits, and shirts that needed the washerwoman; and one officer was seen to spit in a marked manner when the national tricolor was carried beside him.

The large regiment of Château Vieux was in the month of August, 1790 (only one month after the grand oath-swearing in the Champ de Mars), in a very bad humor, and justly so; for while another regiment had been paid three gold louis per man, Château

Vieux got the "cat-o-nine-tails." Another regiment, that called "du Roi," got hold of its money-chest, but for some reason did not break it open.

An inspector, named Malseigne, was sent down by the Assembly to inquire into the soldiers' grievances, and, as far as he could, to rectify them. He was a big, strong man, and brave enough, but he had not much tact; and so it happened that his bluff, bullying manner led him into all sorts of troubles at Nanci. The men of the Château Vieux shut him up in the barrack court where he was holding his inspection, with cries of "Decide it at once!" He got angry, drew his sword, and tried to break through the crowd. He broke his sword, seized another, wounded a sentry, and got out. He retired to a house, the soldiers following. He shut the door, got out the back way, and reached the Town-hall in safety. Next day he tried again to settle the matters of the Château Vieux, but none would listen. Then he ordered them to leave Nanci, but they refused. He then summoned the National Guards to his aid, and by Saturday four thousand had arrived. Still the regiment would not march as ordered. " Pay us," they said, "and we will march to the world's end."

About noon that day, Malseigne escaped from Nanci to Luneville, where there was, he knew, a loyal regiment of Carbineers. He was chased by about a hundred soldiers; but he reached the loyal regiment, and ordered them to fire at his pursuers. The Nanci soldiers, being fired on, rode back again and spread the alarm. " The Carbineers are sold to the Austrians," cried they. Whereupon the three Nanci regiments rose up as one man, and marched to Luneville. A parley followed, and matters were explained. Inspector Malseigne was given up, and marched back to Nanci; but lo! the big man broke away, and was off like a shot, and escaped with only one bullet in his coat. He made a wide, wheeling flight, and returned to the Carbineers, who gave him up a second time; and the next day the mutinous soldiers put him in prison, whither they had also placed Denoue, the com-

"THE DETERMINED OFFICER SAT ON THE TOUCH-HOLE."

mandant of Nanci. When Bouillè heard of these daring acts of rebellion, — of a government inspector and a leading officer in prison,
and three regiments in open mutiny, — he thought a decisive blow ought
to be struck at once. He had a much smaller force than that of the
mutineers, but he had law on his side. When he reached the village
of Frouarde, he sent this message: "You must submit in twenty-four
hours, or I shall make war upon you."

A deputation of soldiers from the mutinous regiments, and one
from the civil authorities of Nanci, went out to Bouillè in the course
of the day. The soldiers, however, were stubborn and even insolent,
but they did not move the general. He insisted on total surrender,
or he would storm Nanci. Distracted were the citizens, distracted
were the soldiers; the regiment of Château Vieux being for resistance
unto death, the others for giving in to Bouillè.

At half-past two the terrible Bouillè was about a mile and a half
from the city gates, and another deputation went forth to meet him.
He granted an hour's respite. Nothing coming of it, the terrified citizens could see the faces of his advanced guard, only thirty paces off.
A flag of truce was then carried forth, and an offer of submission
made.

Now, while the victorious Bouillè was arranging how the mutinous
regiments should leave the city, a very dreadful thing happened. In
the city were many, both citizens and soldiers, who looked upon
Bouillè as a traitor, and were therefore opposed to the surrender.
These men got hold of some loaded cannon, and levelled them
through the gateway at Bouillè's army. A young captain, seeing
lighted matches were being brought to the cannon, flung himself in
front of the mouth of one, and swore that if they did fire it the discharge
should blow him to atoms; and when he was pulled away from the
cannon-mouth by a number of soldiers, the determined officer sat on
the touch-hole. This time the frantic soldiers were not content with
dragging him off his perch; they shot him down as he sat there on

the touch-hole, and then applied a match to the priming. The can-non roared, and fifty men of Bouillè's yanguard were killed. Oh, the rage of the men outside! With levelled bayonet and many a furious oath they dashed through the gate, and then was seen a terrible car-nage. Friend killed friend by mistake that day, for all were so mixed up that it was often difficult to know who were fighting for Bouillè and who were fighting against him. Another cannon, ready loaded, was rendered harmless by a ready-witted woman, who threw a bucket of water on the priming. When the awful scrimmage was over, half the mutinous Château Vieux were found stretched on a gory bed, and many National Guards who fought with them. Bouillè's losses, too, were great. By the time he reached the great Square he was minus forty officers and five hundred men, which shows how obstinately the city was defended, and at what a cost he won his victory.

The mutinous regiments, now shattered and subdued, had to march, each on its appointed route, and peace was restored for a time.

Paris was fearfully agitated by the news, and a solemn funeral ser-vice was held for the slain. The Assembly voted thanks to Bouillè by a great majority; but the lowest ranks of the people, to the number of forty thousand, assembled under the windows of the Riding School, and demanded that the slain mutineers should be avenged.

Whether Bouillè was right or whether he was wrong, he at least quelled in military fashion the spirit of mutiny, and made the whole French army feel that it had at least one captain who could maintain discipline, without which an army is only an armed mob. We mourn over the death of so many brave Frenchmen, but we cannot help admiring the iron determination of General Bouillè in doing what he believed to be his duty.

CHAPTER X.

THE DEATH OF MIRABEAU.

AS long as Mirabeau lived, the king had a friend on whom he could depend. It pleased God, however, to remove this great man when he seemed to be of the utmost use to the French monarchy. When he saw men were going too far and too fast in the direction of changing all the old order, he became a check on their wheels; and he was so mighty in deed and word that it may be truly said he upheld for some time with his one hand the tottering throne.

But he did it at the expense of his strength, and he died, worn out by his immense exertions. No one who had not lived with him and seen him at work could imagine what Mirabeau was able to do in a day. Some one once said to him that such and such things were impossible; when he started up and exclaimed, "Never speak that brute of a word to me any more."

We cannot now follow every step of this great Frenchman, nor understand all he meant to do and would have done had his life been spared. We do know, however, that he was most anxious to remove Louis from the Tuileries.

One night he met the queen in the garden of St. Cloud, and talked over this important matter. She was far more resolute than her royal husband. She was a daughter of the famous Theresa of Austria, and had inherited some of her lofty qualities. In fact, as Mirabeau said of the queen, "She is the only man his Majesty has about him." Louis lacked decision, — he never could make up his mind; and he dreaded above all things a civil war. But no civil war could have been so terrible as the French Revolution proved to be. Had the king left Paris as Mirabeau advised, and flung abroad his banner and rallied his loyal subjects, and put down, as he might have done, the lawless spirit that was abroad, and had he then resolved to rule his people in righteousness, by the advice of the wisest men in France, his reign might have been glorious instead of disastrous, and when he died the criers might have gone about the saddened streets sounding their bells and saying, " Le bon roi Louis, père du peuple, est mort." But it was not in Louis to take this decided step in time. He waited and waited, and then ran away in a clumsy fashion, and, after being stopped at Varennes, he was brought back to Paris in disgrace

The health of Mirabeau had been much impaired by the excessive labors he underwent in managing the affairs of the nation during those most stormy times. The month of March in the year 1791 had arrived. Matters were getting worse instead of better. Duels were being daily fought between the members of the French Parliament, and deadly anger glowed between those who loved the king and those who loved him not. One such duel we will notice, as it shows how the people sided with their champions. A man named Lameth was a prominent leader of the people. He fought the Duke de Castries with swords. As Lameth was making a lunge at the duke's body, his own sword-arm ran against the point of the duke's sword, and was frightfully ripped open. The duel was over, and the people's friend was nearly dead. When the fight ended, the people attacked the duke's house, and flung all his furniture, pictures, and valuables into the street. But not a single thing was stolen ; for this order went about: " The man who steals even a nail shall be hanged."

But to return to the dying Mirabeau. In the month of March, 1791, his strength was evidently giving way. As far back as the January before he was obliged, when he came to the Assembly, to wear linen cloths about his neck, and after the morning debate was over, to apply leeches to his head. He said one day to a friend about this time: "I am dying; I feel as if I were being burned up by a slow fire. When I am gone, they will know how much I was worth."

Things went on thus until the end of March, when the great senator got worse. On the 27th of that month, as he was on his way to the Assembly, he was forced to rest at a friend's house, lying for some time on a sofa in a half-conscious state. When he had recovered, he went to the debate, and spoke no less than five times with all his old fiery energy. He then left the tribune (that is, the speaker's pulpit), and never was seen in it any more. It was Mirabeau's last effort to do what good he could for his distracted country.

Though his popularity had been waning because he opposed the wild schemes of such ignorant quacks as Robespierre, yet, when he was laid in the last days of March on his death-bed, there was hardly a man in Paris who did not feel that his end was a lamentable event. The meanest men in the city jostled against the highest at the door-step, to ask how Mirabeau was. The people of their own free will blocked the street, and allowed no carriage to rattle by and so disturb the sufferer; and every three hours an account of his health was given by the doctors, copied out, printed on hand-bills, and circulated all over Paris.

The second day of April came. It was a Saturday, and the dying man felt sure that he should not live to see the sun rise any more. "I wish," said he to some one who was supporting his head in his last struggle, — "I wish I could leave it to you." After the power of speech had left him, he motioned for a pen and paper, and wrote the word "Opium." The doctor said, "No." Mirabeau wrote next the word "Dormir," and pointed to it. At half-past eight in the morning the end came, and the greatest of Frenchmen had left his country bereft of his wisdom.

A great gloom and a strange silence fell upon the gay and busy city. Every theatre was closed while Mirabeau lay unburied; and wherever the people heard the sounds of music and singing, they knocked loudly at the door, and insisted on the party being broken up at once.

In every street during the next few days you might see men here and there, standing and proclaiming with loud voices and sorrowful faces the virtues and services of the dead statesman. The public funeral, which took place on Monday, the 4th of April, was one of the most wonderful ever seen. The procession itself was three miles in length. It was five o'clock on a sunny April afternoon when Mirabeau was thus carried to his long home, through crowds esti- mated by the hundred thousand. National Guards in double file lined the route, and the deep silence was every now and then broken by the rolling of drums. At the Church of St. Eustache the procession halted to hear a funeral oration ; and when the speaker had finished, the National Guards discharged their muskets in the church, and the vibration caused portions of the roof to fall. It was almost midnight before the great burial was done, and Mirabeau was left sleeping among the worthies of France in the Church of St. Geneviève.

It is painful to think how the Paris mob afterward took up his remains and cast them out in dishonor. This was done by the people in July, 1793, when they buried their apostle Marat where Mirabeau had been laid. Mirabeau did not please the men who adored Marat. Mirabeau was by birth a noble, and, though a great reformer of abuses and a remodeller of the rotten old constitution, he was one who tried to set up the ancient monarchy on a new and firmer basis, and for this he was hated by the more violent party. And when, as we shall see, the iron chest which the king and the blacksmith made in the Tuil- eries was discovered and its papers examined, Mirabeau's share in the attempts to get the king removed from Paris was found out, and his bust in the hall of the Jacobin Club was shivered to atoms by a man who mounted a ladder and hurled it to the ground.

THE DEATH OF MIRABEAU.

So died, so was buried, Gabriel Honoré Mirabeau, a most illustrious man, who crushed the old nobility, as a privileged class, with one hand, while he kept down the madness of the people with the other. He was always a favorite with women, and even the rough fishwives would mount the gallery steps and listen with delight to his speeches; and he was called by them always "Our little mother Mirabeau."

CHAPTER XI.

THE KING'S FLIGHT.

THE king, who had not been very well in the spring of 1791, decided on keeping the festival of Easter at the Palace of St. Cloud. The proposed plan was published with a good deal of parade, as though he wished his subjects to take particular notice of it; which they did, in a very disagreeable manner. For when the day of his little jaunt arrived, and the old family coach, with its eight horses, rolled up to the grand entrance of the Tuileries, the bell of St. Roche pealed out its notes of alarm, and a crowd assembled with the rapidity of wild-fire to stop his Majesty's journey. In vain the king appealed to his loving subjects to let him go. In vain did General Lafayette fret and strive. It would not do. The king should keep his Easter at Paris and nowhere else. For one hour and three quarters did this strange contest go on; and then Louis had to give way, and descend crestfallen from his coach, feeling now that he was indeed a captive. This was on the 18th of April, just one fortnight after Mirabeau's funeral.

The king felt excessively mortified at this treatment, and nursed the plan of escape day and night from thenceforth. As it had now become a difficult matter to get away, he was determined to do it, and without much loss of time.

The queen does not seem to have acted very wisely in her preparations for the great event. As she was about to leave Paris, she thought it necessary to order a vast number of dresses and other toilet matters which she thought she could not live without; and so she managed to keep suspicion on the alert. A lady in her suite, who was a friend of the people, whispered her secrets to General Gouvion, second in command of the National Guard; and he looked the more carefully to his sentries, and kept a yet sharper watch on every carriage which came in or went out of the Tuileries.

Some rooms in the palace which had been occupied by a certain duke were now empty, the duke having emigrated in a pet; and as they had a convenient door of egress, the queen occupied them, intending to slip out when the important moment arrived. There was a certain Swedish count, named Fersen, who had much to do with the king's flight. He got a new coach built big enough to carry the whole royal family, a lot of luggage, and several Body Guards. He told the coachmaker that it was for a Russian baroness, and it was built accordingly, the count being very particular about its construction. This great lumbering affair did not come near the Tuileries, as it might have aroused the suspicion of the sentries on duty. An ordinary glass coach waited on the night of June 20, not far from the palace. The coachman on the box was none other than Count Fersen. By and by a lady with a hood, and two children, wearing hoods also, came from the duke's door into the court, and thence into the street, and entered the coach. Then came another lady, followed by a gentleman in a round hat, and they got in also, but the coachman still waited. Now the suspicious lady of the bedchamber had her own reasons for supposing the royal family meant to escape that very night; and she told Gouvion, and he told Lafayette, and Lafayette came himself in his carriage to see with his own eyes whether all was well or not at the Tuileries. Now the general's carriage, driven at a rapid pace and glaring with lamps, passed so close to a lady in a broad-brimmed gypsy hat, that she was able to touch one of its wheels with a light stick which she held in her hand. That lady was Marie Antoinette, the Queen of France. Somewhat flurried by the noise and lights of Lafayette's carriage, the queen, as she went to the glass coach that was waiting, took the wrong turn instead of the right one. · A servant attended her; but the stupid man did not know his way about, and·he and the queen wandered about the streets until they had wasted one precious hour. What must the gentleman in the round hat have felt all this time? For he was the king, and the two children were his children, and one of the ladies was his sister.

And how the count on the box must have fretted at the delay! But at length the queen appeared, and stepped in; the stupid servant got up behind, the count cracked his whip, and they were off. The poet in "John Gilpin" says, —

> "The stones did rattle underneath,
> As if Cheapside were mad;"

and, surely, not less did the stones of the Rue de Grammont rattle, as the royal family of France were borne away rapidly toward the Russian lady's big new coach. Before long it was in sight, waiting there with its six horses; and in a few moments the gentleman in the round hat, the lady in the gypsy bonnet, and the others were seated in it. As for the glass coach, the count turned it round, and left it to its fate, and it was found the next morning in the ditch. The count jumped on the box of the new carriage he had been so anxious about, cracked his whip, and made the six horses go as fast as they could; but the progress was dolefully small. The new coach travelled only sixty-nine miles in twenty-two hours.

When Count Fersen had done his part, he made a low bow, and took his leave; and on went the king's new coach with its six horses, another chaise behind with a pair, and three couriers in yellow, each astride of a nag, making a cavalcade of eleven horses in all. What an unwise display! Now and then there was something amiss with the harness, and delays occurred; and when the huge machine had to be dragged up a hill, the king got out and walked. General Bouillè had soldiers stationed here and there along the route, and every-

DROUET COMPARING THE FACE ON THE ASSIGNAT WITH THE FACE UNDER
THE ROUND HAT.

thing was done which seemed best; but the whole affair was mismanaged, and ended in grievous failure.

At a village named St. Menehould there lived at that time an old soldier named Drouet. He had retired from service, and was master of the post there. He was a stanch patriot (as the favorers of the revolution were then called), and on that eventful night he happened to be in a very bad temper because some one had interfered with his privileges. Toward sunset the great coach rumbled into the village, attracting by its splendor everybody's notice, and especially that of the old soldier Drouet. His suspicions were at once aroused; and while the royal party were halting, he scanned carefully the side face of the gentleman inside, and thought he had seen him before somewhere. Was it in the Champ de Mars last July?

"Fetch me a new assignat," said he to some one near. An assignat was a sort of bank-note, with the king's head engraved on it. Drouet had no sooner compared the face on the assignat with the face under the round hat than he felt quite sure the gentleman was the king, attempting to escape.

As quick as thought Drouet told his mind to another old dragoon, and they two, mounting swift-footed horses, were off, having first whispered a word to the village authorities to rouse what National Guards and patriot men there might be in St. Menehould. Off then rode the two old dragoons, and after a rough night-ride reached Varennes before the king and his party had succeeded in leaving it. Bouillè's son was here to receive them; but the foolish young fellow, thinking all was over for the night, had gone to bed. While the king was trying to get fresh horses, a good half-hour was wasted, and during that half-hour Drouet and his comrade had reached the village and stopped the king's progress. They had found a light still burning in the Golden Arm Inn; and the landlord, whose name was Le Blanc, was serving guests. Entering in, Drouet called the landlord aside, and asked, "Art thou a good patriot?" Le Blanc said, "I am;" and then Drouet whispered his story in his ear. Then, while Le Blanc bestirred himself in his own way, the two old soldiers went out and blocked the road by overturning a furniture van, and by adding to it such other things as barrows, barrels, and the like. Le Blanc by this time had brought his brother and one or two other patriots; and the party then stood, muskets in hand, awaiting the arrival of the king and his cavalcade. When the coach reached the place, its way was barred. It had to stop, and at the same moment the barrels of two guns were thrust into the coach windows, and a gruff voice demanded passports. There was no further advance to be thought of; no friendly aid was near; no young Bouillè and his troopers; nothing was to be done but to stay the remainder of the short night in the village. The baffled royal party put up at a grocer's shop, where they were served with bread and cheese and a bottle of burgundy.

Thus was the king taken captive, and so did his attempted flight come to an inglorious end. About seven o'clock on Saturday night the great coach might have been seen returning to Paris. The king was carried through a vast crowd of silent and wondering citizens, who had been instructed by a widely circulated placard how to behave on the occasion. "Whoever insults Louis shall be caned," it said; "and whoever applauds him shall be hanged."

CHAPTER XII.

A YEAR AFTER THE KING'S FLIGHT.

WHEN the king was brought back to the Tuileries, he was at first watched more closely than before. Even outside the bedroom door a sentinel was stationed; and one night, when the queen could not sleep, a National Guard offered to sit by her bedside and have a little chat with her.

But in a while the king's friends had contrived to surround him with eighteen hundred loyal men, selected from various districts of France, all under command of the Duke de Brissac. Beside these, Louis had his Swiss Guards stationed in or about the palace. By and by, too, the flight to Varennes seemed more or less forgotten, and Lafayette obtained a general amnesty; that is, a forgiveness of all past faults on all sides. The king and queen might now be seen sometimes at the Opera; and *vivats* — that is, cheers — were sometimes raised as the royal equipage rolled through the streets. On the 30th of September the old Assembly was dissolved, after sitting nearly twenty-nine months, and a new one began its labors the next day. The streets were illuminated, and two very popular deputies named Robespierre and Pétion were carried home on men's shoulders amid much shouting. So the twelve hundred who had met in the Tennis Court, and there had vowed-to complete their work in spite of all, were broken up and went their ways.

The new Parliament consisted of seven hundred and forty-five men, and they were mostly of a patriot turn of mind. No less than four hundred of them were lawyers. The king had some friends in this

Parliament, but they were lovers of liberty too. The extreme revolutionary men sat on the left side of the president, on some benches high up, and so got the name of "The Men of the Mountain."

The country, though fairly quiet upon the whole, was in an explosive state, and a riot broke out every now and then. La Vendée had to be carefully watched all the winter long by General Dumouriez, a very able soldier. The Mayor of Étampes, who hung out a red flag (the same as reading the Riot Act), was trampled to death. As for the navy and army, they were in a wretched state; and the law was slack to punish crime. The king's party worked very hard to keep up an appearance of loyalty. Some of the leading Republicans (Danton, for instance) were hushed by presents of money; and men were actually hired to applaud the king when he appeared in public. Some of the lowest of the Paris populace were also hired to applaud speeches favorable to the king in the Assembly. Men, too, were paid to "write up" the monarchy. The king's friends who had emigrated hoped, of course, for the restoration of the past. It was said that Coblentz had become a second Versailles; for there the princes and nobles chiefly gathered and enrolled themselves in a little army, ready when the time came to invade France and punish the rebellious people; and letters written in cipher frequently passed to and fro between these emigrants outside France and the king's friends at home. A certain newspaper called the "Friend of the King" (*Ami du Roi*) was able to name the number of those who were biding their time for the invasion of France. There were, according to that paper, four hundred and nineteen thousand foreign soldiers and fifteen thousand emigrants. All this was enough to incense highly the French people; for they knew if the king's foreign friends came down on them, they would be punished horribly for behaving as they had to their sovereign. It was therefore a very anxious time for both people and ruler.

In the month of June, 1792, the Duke of Brunswick declared openly that it was high time to march on Paris and deliver Louis from his troubles. A camp of twenty thousand national volunteers was thereupon decreed by the French Government for the needful defence of the city, each man to be a picked patriot. It was also decreed that the priests, as presumed friends of the king and favorers of Brunswick, should be banished. What did the king now do? He placed his veto (" I forbid ") on each of these decrees. He was remonstrated with by Roland, the Minister of the Interior, in a very plain letter; but the king stuck to his veto, and all his ministers resigned in consequence. This happened on the 13th of June, 1792. Both the decrees were hateful to the king, for he knew the twenty thousand volunteers would be violent Jacobins, and the priests were his friends; and so he said " Veto " to both. But as he did it he was pulling the house down upon his head; he was raising a storm which swept him from the palace to the prison of the Temple.

Paris was now in a state of frenzy. The Duke of Brunswick was just about to march, and yet the king forbade their raising a garrison of twenty thousand patriots for the defence of their homes and wives. It was now that every patriot who had the courage of a man screwed that courage to the sticking-point, and resolved to do or die. One deputy after another came to the Parliament to entreat it to alter the king's power of veto. It was now that Barbaroux, a fiery South-countryman, wrote to Marseilles for " six hundred men who knew how to die! "

The 20th of June arrived; it had already become a memorable day, for it was the anniversary of the Tennis Court Oath. Some of the citizens of Paris had resolved to celebrate the day by planting a tree of liberty near the Tuileries, and by also, perhaps, having a word or two with the king himself, if they could see him, on the subject of the veto.

On the morning of this eventful day the tree of liberty was ready. It was a Lombardy poplar, and it was lying quietly on a sort of car, ready to be moved when the time came. The authorities, fearful of riot and bloodshed, attempted to stop the affair; but the people assured them that they had the most peaceful intentions, and only wished to plant a tree and have a word with their king. So the procession set forward, each moment swelled by hundreds from every alley and court of the suburb of St. Antoine. A curious banner was borne aloft. It was no less than a pair of old black silk breeches, with these words as a motto in French: "Tremble, tyrants! here are the Sansculottes!" (Sansculotte was a cant name given to the poorest patriots by the Royalists; it means "destitute of breeches.")

Once more the authorities tried to stop the crowd; but the leaders answered them: "We are as peaceable as doves; we mean no harm. We cannot stop now; and you would better come with us." And so the patriot stream followed on until it reached the Riding School, where the Parliament was met for business. Here an address was read; and then the multitude surrounded the palace, all the gates of which had been carefully closed. Within the courts were ranked the National Guards. The Swiss were at their posts, and the palace itself was crowded with Royalists in black clothes, who had come to support their king. Every man of this sort had a "ticket of entry," which he showed to the sentinel at the gate.

The Lombardy poplar was planted, — not where they wished, for the place was closed, but in a garden not far off; and now, as the king would not come out to them, they resolved to force their way in to him. In this they were helped by the National Guards inside. Those men, never very loyal, yielded to the speech of the mob leaders, and opened the gate. The multitude poured through, and were soon surging up the grand stairs into the interior of the Tuileries. It was a repetition of the insurrection of women at Versailles. Loud were the knockings on the door behind which the poor distracted monarch stood, — knockings that could not be overlooked, for soon the panels were smashed in. Louis opened the door and asked them hastily, "What do you want here?" Loud shouts of "Veto!" "Remove the

THE QUEEN PUTTING THE RED CAP ON HER LITTLE SON'S HEAD.

veto!" answered his question. Others shouted, "Bring back the patriot ministers!" Louis answered with much dignity, " This is not the time to do it in, nor is this the proper way to ask me."

A few soldiers managed to get the king into the bow of a window, and there he stood for some time. One man thrust a red cap into his hand, and he set it upon his head. Another offered him a bottle, and he put it to his lips. The queen sat in an inner room with her children and sister-in-law, behind a barricade of tables, in tears and terror of heart. And this went on for fully three hours. The gentlemen had all disappeared, fearful of doing more harm than good to the king's cause. After a time the Mayor of Paris (Pétion was his name), a very advanced patriot who had just now much influence with the mob, persuaded the people to retire. They obeyed his voice; and as they passed through the room where the queen sat behind her tables, a woman presented her with a red cap, which she put on her little son's head. It was not until eight o'clock that the palace was clear of the people, and the king and queen, much agitated, were able to embrace each other with many tears after enduring such terrors.

CHAPTER XIII.

THE MARSEILLESE.

AFTER the king had attempted to escape on the longest day in the year 1791, many were the stormy debates in the French Parliament on the subject. The question uppermost for a time was, "What are we to do with the monarchy?" Some answered briefly and bluntly, "Do with it? Why, do away with it." "Do with it?" asked the Royalists. "Preserve it at any cost;" and, for the present, the advice of the Royalists was followed, and the "Men of the Mountain" were silenced. But yet from all parts of France there came petitions that the monarch should be deposed; and one very urgent body of patriots came all the way from Marseilles to beg that the king, who ran away like a naughty boy from school, should no longer sit on the throne. One of these fiery speakers said these remarkable words: "When our ancestors landed on the coast of France and founded our city long ago, they flung a bar of iron into the bay. Now, this bar shall float again on the waves of the Mediterranean Sea before we, the people of Marseilles, will consent to be slaves."

The National Assembly, however, having decided on the 15th of July — that is, about three weeks after the king's return — that the monarchy should not be abolished, the hot-tempered men of Marseilles went about their business; but it became clear from that time what side they would take, when the great question of king or no king came to be decided.

And, as we have seen, when the king in the next June refused to allow two decrees of Parliament, — one about the banishment of priests, and the other about the levying of twenty thousand patriots for the defence of Paris, — a certain member, named Barbaroux, remembering the fiery temper of the deputation from Marseilles, wrote to the mayor of that city, and begged him to send to Paris "six hundred men who knew how to die" (*qui savent mourir*).

The letter was carried in the leather post-bag by the slow-going diligence, and in due time reached Marseilles. The six hundred men who knew how to die came forth, and were duly enrolled and armed, and on the 5th of July they began their long march. The authorities of the town said to them, "March, and strike down the tyrant;" and with these orders they went their way, musket on shoulder and sword on thigh. They also dragged after them two pieces of cannon, not knowing what might happen. Many other men, bound on the same errand, were wending their way to Paris about this time, being invited by the National Assembly, who contemplated the holding of another such gathering as we saw before in the Champ de Mars, when there were such preparations and such rejoicing. But while those went by twos and threes or twenties or thirties, it was Marseilles alone which sent forth a little army of "six hundred men who knew how to die."

On this mass of Southern fire and valor the eyes of all men were soon fastened. It was for them that the wonderful tune called "The Marseillaise" was composed and set to suitable words. The happy composer of this most noble song was a certain colonel, named Rouget de Lisle, who long survived the stormy period of the Revolution, and who was alive as late as 1836. Those of our readers who have never heard this tune, or have heard it without knowing the story of its composition, should get some good pianoforte-player to play it, and then let them say whether it is not a tune to "make the blood tingle in their veins," as Carlyle says.

The "six hundred men who knew how to die" left Marseilles, as we have said, on the 5th of July. On the 14th was the feast on the Champ de Mars, but the Marseillese were not in time for that. It was a sad feast, unworthy of the name. The place was bright with sunshine, and the people were there in abundance, and the king went, and there were trees of liberty and bands of music; but as for Louis, no man said, " God bless him!" The popular man of the hour was Pétion, the Mayor of Paris, who had been dismissed by the king's friends and restored again. Chalked on men's hats were the words " Vive Pétion!" " Pétion or Death!" Some were afraid that the king would be murdered ; and he himself was not without fear of it, for he went to the Champ de Mars with bullet-proof armor under his waistcoat.

On the 22d of July, being Sunday, the Assembly proclaimed the country to be in danger. The same sad story, " La patrie est en danger!" was emblazoned on a large banner, and it was cried aloud by heralds with sound of trumpet. And now, in spite of the royal " veto " upon enlistment of volunteers, and in answer to the mournful tidings " Our country is in danger!" hundreds of young men might be seen that Sunday afternoon enrolling their names in a book in every section of Paris. As each volunteer signed his name, there was a shout of " Vive la patrie!" and sounds of weeping from some who were rejected because they were too small. In a day or two ten thousand were on their way to Soissons, where a camp was formed.

On July 25 the Duke of Brunswick, with thirty thousand foot and ten thousand horse, struck his tents, and marched on Paris. He had many emigrants in his ranks. He said in his proclamation what he meant to do for France. He meant to restore the king, and to hang everybody who resisted him, and to reduce Paris, if she would not submit, to a heap of rubbish.

This proclamation inflamed the minds of the French people yet more, and made them resolve to do what they had to do with all their might.

It was now felt by all patriots that the time had come to pluck the king from his place, and put him under lock and key or in the silent

YOUNG MEN ENROLLING THEIR NAMES.

tomb. He was, as they thought, the cause of this invasion of their country; and there is no doubt that an insurrection on a large scale was now being organized in Paris with as much secrecy as possible. It was, however, not to take place until after the arrival of the " six hundred who knew how to die." These men had been marching day by day upon the dusty roads of France ever since the 5th of July, and they were now drawing nigh the " tyrant " whom they had been .sent to " strike down." As the crow flies, Paris may be distant from Marseilles about four hundred and eighty miles; by road it is more. On the 29th of July the six hundred were at Charenton, where several leading patriots met them, and where they were entertained with a dinner at the Blue Dial. On the 30th they made a grand public entry into Paris, and were met by the Jacobin Club in a body on the site of the fallen Bastille. Having with some difficulty forced their way through the crowded streets, they reached the Hôtel de Ville, where Mayor Pétion welcomed them and received their mus-kets. They then marched on to a tavern, where a plain repast was prepared for them.

This dinner was not fated to be eaten in peace, for the arrival of the six hundred was noised abroad, and, of course, much detested by the Royalists. A certain loyal body of National Guards, formed of rich and respectable men from a wealthy quarter of Paris, hap-pened to be on guard at the Tuileries the same day; and these men, or part of them who were off duty for a while, chanced to be dining not far from the tavern where the six hundred were about to dine. These Nationals had dined, and were strolling about, when they were hooted by some of the mob who had followed the Mar-seillese. Words begat blows; and as some of the Nationals drew their swords, the mob cried out, " Help, men of Marseilles! " The six hun-dred had not yet sat down to their meal, and, hearing the cries, they opened the tavern windows, and leaped out, drawing their swords at the same time. The Nationals, not liking the looks of such fierce fellows, retired, at first face to face with the foe, but, finding this would not do, they wheeled round and fled.   Quick over the Tuileries draw-bridge or into the muddy ditch they sprang.   One man, too stout to fly, got a blow from the flat of a sword; others were cut or pricked in the back; and another, who had twice fired a pistol at his pursuers and missed them all, was run through and died on the spot.   Such sad events happened on the first day spent by the six hundred in Paris. They evidently knew how to kill as well as how to die.

The great crisis was clearly drawing nigh.   More and more loudly came the clamor for deposing the king.   The galleries of the Assem-bly were now crammed with excited women, or men waving swords, and interrupting the debate with shouts of " Depose the king ! "

On the 3d of August the Mayor Pétion and all the Council came and openly petitioned for it; every patriot wished it, and the Assembly could do nothing until they had promised to consider the question on the 9th of the same month.

On Sunday, the 5th, the king held a levee at the Tuileries.   It was his last !   Never for a long time had one been so crowded.   Out-side the palace, within a few steps, the restless city was all astir, de-manding in every street the deposition of the king.   Inside, a last, but fruitless attempt was being made to carry the king away to Rouen; but the undecided monarch would not seize his last chance of escape.

" No," said he ; " I believe the insurrection is not so near as you think."

But he was fatally mistaken, as we shall see.

CHAPTER XIV

THE SWISS GUARD.

IT will be remembered that the palace of the King of France was guarded by a thousand Swiss soldiers. These men were well drilled, brave, and faithful; and even in the raging sea of disloyal Paris the monarch felt secure, — too secure, as it proved. The Swiss do not seem to have meddled with the politics of the day, but to have done their duty, earned their paltry pay, and kept to themselves.

We have already noticed the king's Sunday levee, and the futile efforts which his friends made to get him removed to Rouen. These he would not second; "for," said he, "the insurrection is not so near as you suppose." But it was near, very near now. In fact, the leaders of the Revolution had already determined that if the Assembly would not pronounce the dethronement of Louis on the next Thursday, they would rise and do it by force of arms.

But the Assembly were busied about Lafayette, who had denounced the Jacobins, by a letter, as dangerous people; his conduct was therefore discussed for several days, and on Wednesday he was acquitted of blame by a majority of two to one.

Thursday evening arrived, and no sentence of deposition had been pronounced. All that night men were arming and drilling, and making ready for an attack on the Tuileries early the next morning. The loyal gentlemen of France were aware that something serious was about to happen; and they gathered round their king, each man with his weapon of war. It was a very close night, and the palace windows were thrown open, for every room was densely crowded. About midnight those in the palace could plainly hear the "storm-bells" calling the people together in various parts of the city. One bell was the same which was rung by a king's order on St. Bartholomew's Eve, 1572, as a signal for the massacre of the Huguenots. Another bell which sounded in the night air was that of the Town-hall; this was pulled by Marat, the editor of the "People's Friend," who had been imprisoned for what he had written.

It must have been an awful night; and yet as its hours stole on and no armed mobs appeared, a joke was bandied from one to the other: "The tocsin is like a dry cow; it does not yield any milk."

During the night the king had a short nap, and about five o'clock he went out into the garden to review his troops, in company with old Marshal Maillé, who was nearly eighty years of age. The soldiers did not seem very loyal, and their shouts of "Vive le Roi" ended in "Vive la Nation," — as if the king and nation were not one and the same, as they ought to be.

When the sun began to shine, a countless army of men who had been gathering, each in his proper quarter during the night, united and moved in the direction of the Tuileries. At the head of all, in the place of honor, marched the "six hundred who knew how to die." There were squadrons drawn up to resist this army of the people, but none of them did anything except get quietly out of the road; so that the six hundred and the host which followed in their rear found no resistance until they arrived at the outer gate of the great courtyard of the palace, called the Place du Carrousel.

If Louis had been a general, like Napoleon, or even if he had been a resolute prince like Charles the First, he might have made a good fight of it, and even carried the day. It is said that the queen offered him a pistol and said, "Now, if ever, it is the time for you to show yourself a hero." But Louis was not a fighting man. He did not lack courage, but he lacked the resolution to strike one great blow for his ancient crown. There he sat in this awful hour doing nothing; his hands were on his knees, and his head bent low. The troops in the court sent in for orders. " Are we to fire the cannon on the people or not?" No orders were sent out to them; so they threw down their lighted matches. There was no head; no quick, sharp word of command; no orders promptly given and as promptly obeyed. A few minutes after eight o'clock the king decided on leaving the palace and taking refuge in the Assembly. He left his gallant gentlemen and his red-coated Switzers to fight or yield, to fly or die, as they liked or could. There they were left; and they turned their reproachful looks on the monarch who had abandoned them, until he and his queen and children were lost to sight in the crowd. The gentlemen slipped away as well as they were able by one door or another, and the unfortunate Swiss Guard stood to their arms and waited what might happen like brave men. They were soon face to face with the six hundred, and then there was a short parley.

" Where is the king?"

" He has gone over to the Assembly."

" We have come here to take possession of his house until the Assembly pronounces him deposed."

And then what were the Swiss Guard to do or say, the king having gone? Were they to defend the empty palace or not? While pausing undecided, there was a discharge of cannon, and the balls struck the roof of the Tuileries. This seems to have decided the Swiss captain. " Fire!" said he.

His men did so; and not a few Marseillese lay stretched on the earth, dead or dying, the next moment. The volley was so sudden and well-directed, and the appearance of the serried ranks of the Swiss so terrible, that the huge mob recoiled, and backed out of the great court, and the Swiss advancing seized the cannon and prepared to use them in their own defence.

The "six hundred who knew how to die" soon rallied, however, and returned to the charge; and the National Guards in the garden

also fired on the Swiss as foreigners while they were attempting,
though without success, to discharge the cannon. Had they succeeded in firing off those great guns, the cause of the king might
not have been lost. But even though they could not manage the
cannon, they fired their muskets with deadly precision, and killed very
many people. Bonaparte himself was a witness of this battle, and he
believed that the Swiss would have won the day if they had had a
capable general.

When this bloody struggle was at its height, a written order of the
king was carried by some daring messenger to the Swiss to cease firing.
But why did he not also order the mob to cease firing? The poor
Swiss obeyed the order and fired no more, but were fired at as hotly as
ever. What were they now to do? The people had become mad-
dened like bears bereft of their whelps, for they saw bleeding and
dying patriots carried along the streets; and the Swiss felt sure if they
laid down their arms and ventured into the crowd they would be torn
to pieces in a moment. Yet something must be done, and at once;
so they broke up into detachments, and tried to make their way to
places of safety.

One party was utterly destroyed; another rushed into the National
Assembly, and found a refuge there; a third, three hundred strong,
made for the Champs Élysées and Courbevoye, where there were
other soldiers of their nation. But very few of them escaped; they
died fighting here and there. Fifty were marched to the Hôtel de
Ville; but they were massacred on the way, every one. The Marseillese, like brave men, tried to save the Guard after the victory was won;
but the Paris mob were cruel, and thirsted for the last drop of the
Swiss soldiers' blood.

This murder of unresisting men, who had simply done the duty
they were paid to do, is a very dark blot on the character of the people
of Paris. It shows them in a very unfavorable light. But to our
minds it is also a great blot on the king's character; for he forsook his

THE SWISS GUARD FIRING ON THE MARSEILLESE.

brave defenders, and then, by sending an order to cease firing, he became, though without meaning it, their destroyer. They were paid sixpence a day for defending his house, and when it was attacked they acted as true soldiers only could and would have acted; and in obeying the king's orders to cease firing, they became martyrs to the high cause of soldierly discipline. Near Lucerne there is a monumental lion, the work of a first-rate sculptor, which has been erected in memory of these brave men.

The scenes inside the Tuileries were shocking and hardly to be described. Outside, one hundred and eighty bodies of dead Swiss guardsmen were piled in one ghastly heap; while more than a hundred carts, piled up with dead patriots, went sorrowfully away from the scene of bloodshed to the cemetery of Sainte Madeleine.

CHAPTER XV.

AFTER the sack of the Tuileries and the destruction of the Swiss Guard, the king and his family were sent in Mayor Pétion's carriage, not to the palace of the Luxembourg, but to the tower of the Temple, a very gloomy-looking place indeed. Here the king was kept under close observation, and was subjected to many indignities which he must have felt very keenly. How often now he must have wished that he had got away from Paris when such a thing was possible! But he may yet have cherished a hope of being rescued by the Duke of Brunswick and the Austrians. The kings of the countries round about France were highly incensed at the treatment of their brother Louis, and the King of Prussia drew his sword to rescue him from the clutches of the fierce patriots of Paris.

The month of September, 1792, was a very remarkable one. Two things are especially to be noticed in it. One is the gallant manner in which the French people formed themselves into armies, and marched, full of cheerful courage, against the invaders of their country; the other is the murderous hate shown by those in the cities, especially Paris, against the upper classes, whom they regarded as the cause of all their troubles. Let us recall what was done in Paris in this month of September, 1792. On the motion of the president the Assembly was dissolved, and a new National Convention ordered to assemble; and on Sunday, the 2d of September, the electors began to choose their deputies, to the number of seven hundred and forty-four, who were to meet at the Tuileries.

Until they could get together, the country, now left without a government, was guided by the Paris municipals, or Commune, — all men of very revolutionary minds, dressed in tricolor sashes, passing a hundred decrees daily, sitting ever with food in their pockets and loaded pistols always at hand. There were Robespierre, Marat, and others, raging and foaming against the thirty thousand aristocrats of Paris. A new high court of justice was also organized by Danton, with four fiery men from each section. Four days after this court was set up, Dr. Guillotin's new instrument of death began its work. The first victim condemned by the new court and executed by the guillotine was the royalist Collenot d'Angremont. Others followed, and the appetite of Paris for horrors grew daily stronger. On the 28th of August Danton came to the Commune, and asked for a decree to search every house in Paris for arms. He got his decree granted, and two thousand muskets were soon ferreted out, and, more than that, four hundred suspected persons were hurried off to one of the prisons. Guards were stationed at the end of every street, and the door of each house was broken open, if not opened willingly at the dread knock of Danton's officials. A great terror now fell on all the respectable classes of Paris, and every day saw the prisons getting fuller of Royalists.

Dumouriez was now the general of the army; and such an army! — mere raw recruits, almost beggars! On Sunday, September 2, the news came of the arrival of the Duke of Brunswick at Verdun, with sixty thousand men. General Beaurepaire, who held Verdun, blew his brains out with a pistol, because the municipals bade him surrender the place.

The Duke of Brunswick had engaged to dine in Paris on a certain day, and the other kings and powers were advancing; and France was in a state of terror, almost of despair. We must remember all this when we read of the September massacres. No one can find an excuse for murder; but France, and especially Paris, was then as nearly mad as a country can be, with great armies girding her round, and breathing out threats of what they meant to do when they came. What a Sunday that was! — huge posters on the walls; storm-bells sounding; men and women offering to shoulder musket and mount guard! Then it was that Danton made one of his mighty speeches, which set every heart on fire.

So far, so good. But what was Marat doing that Sunday, and cruel Billaud, and others like-minded? No man knows exactly; but it is supposed they had much to do with the fearful scenes which soon afterward steeped this Sunday and the next few days in innocent blood. The infamous massacre of helpless victims began about three o'clock, and in this manner. A number of priests who would not take the oath were being carried in six coaches along the streets to the Abbaye Prison. Many people were standing about cursing the priests to their hearts' content, scowling and shaking their fists at them. Some of the more violent got on the carriage-steps and pulled down the window-blinds, which the priests had drawn up. One of the priests, a man of quick temper, struck one of the mob with a cane. This was a fatal act; for as soon as it was done the carriages were stopped, and the priests dragged out into the street and brutally murdered, close to the prison gate.

This was the beginning of the September massacres, which lasted from that Sunday afternoon until Thursday evening. The dreadful tragedy was enacted in this manner. A rude court of justice was formed in every prison. Before this the prisoners were tried one after another. If they were declared innocent, they were set free with loud cries of "Vive la Nation!" But if, as more frequently was the case, they were doomed by the court, they were liberated at the outer gate, but without the words "Vive la Nation!" They were liberated, indeed, but to what? "The condemned man was conducted," says the historian, "into a howling sea, under an arch of wild sabres, axes, and pikes." He sank, hewn asunder. Then another sank, and another; and there was a heap of corpses.

M. DE SOMBREUIL'S DAUGHTER PLEADING FOR HER FATHER'S LIFE.

Among those who were thus murdered, let us single out one noted for her beauty and virtues, the Princess Lamballe. She had escaped to England at the time when the king made his attempt to get away in the summer of 1791 ; but she returned to die miserably just outside the Abbaye Prison. The princess had thrown herself upon a bed to rest, when one of the prison turnkeys came in and told her that she was to be removed to another place.

" I am well enough here," said she ; " I do not wish to remove."

" But you must."

" Then," said she, " I will arrange my dress a little."

" You will not have far to go," the jailer replied.

The princess was led to the gate. She was not even tried, being so well known a friend of the queen. She was led to the awful gate and pushed forcibly into the street ; for at the sight of what was awaiting her, she shrank back with horror. But there was no help for her; she must go forward into the " howling sea, under the arch of wild sabres, axes, and pikes." Her head was cleft with the cruel axe, and her body was cut in pieces. Her head was then fixed on a pike and carried before the windows of the Temple, that the queen might see it and be agonized at the sight.

Old Monsieur de Sombreuil had a daughter. She pleaded for him in so touching a manner that he was spared ; but one horrible condition was made, — she had to drink aristocrats' blood, to show that she and her father hated aristocrats.

Several very thrilling accounts were written by men who were then in one of the prisons, and who were among the saved ones. Carlyle has given us some account of three of these men ; namely, the Abbé Sicard, Advocate Maton, and Jourgniac. Jourgniac's little book is called " The Agony of Thirty-eight Hours." He speaks of Sunday night in the Abbaye, and how they waited for death hour by hour, " gazing on the pavement of their prison, on which lay the moonlight checkered with the triple stanchions of the windows." At two o'clock, he says: "The Abbé Lenfant and the Abbé de Chapt Rastignac appeared in the pulpit of the chapel which was our prison. They said to us that our end was at hand; that we must compose ourselves, and receive their last blessing. We threw ourselves on our knees and received it. Half an hour afterward they were both massacred, and we heard their cries."

Maton says, among other things: "Baudin de la Chenaye was called. Sixty years of virtues could not save him. He passed the fatal outer gate, gave a cry of terror at the heaped corpses, covered his eyes with his hands, and died of innumerable wounds. About seven o'clock in the morning four men entered with bludgeons and sabres. Four sabres were crossed over my breast, and I was brought to their bar. The judge was a lame man, of tall, lank stature."

Jourgniac gives us an account of the tribunal. The president, in a gray coat, with a sabre at his side, stood leaning with his hands on a table. Some ten persons were around, seated or standing; and two men in bloody shirts guarded the door of the place. While I was being tried, a prisoner was brought in. It was one priest more whom they had ferreted out of the chapel. After a very few questions they said, "A la Force." The priest flung his breviary on the table, and was driven out and massacred. Jourgniac got off, and so did Maton and Sicard; but one thousand and eighty-nine were murdered, and carts went along the streets, filled with human corpses to be buried in the cemeteries. Of these victims two hundred and two were priests. When Danton was taken to task about these and other horrors under his authority as Minister of Justice, he said, "Are they not guilty?" and turned his back on the speaker.

CHAPTER XVI.

THE ENEMY AT BAY.

DUMOURIEZ, now the leader of the French armies, was a brave and able soldier. On the night of August 28 he assembled a council of war at his lodgings at Sedan, and spread a map of France on the table. He heard all that his officers had to say; most of them advising him to retreat to Paris, where something might happen for his advantage. Dumouriez thanked them all, and wished them a good-night; then he called to his private room a certain young officer named Thouvenot.

"See there," said he to Thouvenot, as he pointed to the map of France; "that is the forest of Argonne, a long stretch of rocky mountain and wild wood, with but *five*, or perhaps only *three* passes through it. Might we not seize them?"

On the 29th Dumouriez left Sedan for the forest, and did seize those passes forthwith

The month of September was one of the wettest on record; and the country through which the army of Brunswick toiled toward Paris — a difficult country at all times — was made much more so by reason of the bad weather. The long chain of the Argonne forest stretching forty miles, with but five passes at the most, all occupied by French soldiers, presented a natural rampart which the invaders could not break through. Each pass was blocked with felled trees, and held by desperate men; and how to surmount that obstacle the Bruns-wickers knew not. They tried several times, but failed always. The weather continued wretched, the wood was too green to burn, the sour grapes brought on dysentery, and the peasants of Champagne were, as was likely, very unfriendly, and killed a Brunswicker whenever they could. There was only one way left by which the duke could get to Paris, and that was by going round the end of the mountain chain; and this he did, after losing twenty-five days in trying to force a way through the passes. He now brought his men face to face with the French. Dumouriez had much trouble with his raw recruits. Once there was a panic and a mutiny, as was very natural among young fellows who had just come from Paris. The general had to rate them very soundly, as not worthy of being called soldiers, but scoundrels. Yet these very men were being rapidly manufactured into the best soldiers of that age, — men who, under the orders of the famous captains of the Republic, were ready to go anywhere and do anything.

In the camp of the Duke of Brunswick there was a certain great author named Goethe. He came with a small body of men from Weimar, and he has left behind him his opinions of cannon-balls and such-like things. He likens the sound of cannon-balls to that of the humming of tops or the whistle of birds; and he says that under fire you feel as if you were in some very hot place.

On the 20th of September Kellermann, the second in command under Dumouriez, engaged the Brunswickers in a battle, which raged near the mill of Valmy till seven o'clock. Kellermann's horse was killed, and a powder-magazine blown up, and the enemy thought it a good time to attack; but the "little rascals" of Paris, raw and ragged though they might be, stood like rocks, and shouted, "Vive la Patrie!" and the well-drilled and well-armed foe had to retire in great surprise.

There was a place beyond Metz called Thionville, which at the same time was fiercely battered and besieged, but the people there were equally brave and determined. They made a wooden horse and set him on the battlements of their city, and they hung a bundle of hay before his nose, and they wrote an inscription in large letters,

THE WOODEN HORSE ON THE BATTLEMENTS OF THIONVILLE.

so that the enemy could read it afar off: "When I have eaten my hay, then you will take Thionville."

On the day of the battle at Valmy the new National Convention met in the "Hall of the Hundred Swiss" at the forsaken Tuileries, and proceeded to decree that same afternoon some revolutionary decrees, one of which was this: "Royalty from this day is abolished in France." When the news of this decree reached the French soldiers in Argonne, they stuck their caps on their bayonet-points and shouted "Vive la République!" till the welkin rang again with the noise. The Brunswickers and their allies now retired from the contest, and raised the sieges of Thionville and Lille. At the siege of the latter place the queen's sister, an Austrian archduchess, was present; and the artillery officers, being eager to oblige her with a sight of what great guns can do, overcharged some mortars, which burst and killed thirty men. The Austrians rained balls and bombs on Lille, the latter being filled with oil of turpentine; and they aimed their fire chiefly at the houses of the poor, and spared the rich quarter as much as they could. Many houses in Lille were set on fire, but the poor people nimbly ran about with pails of water helping one another. A certain barber of ready wit caught up a fragment of a splintered bomb, made a shaving-dish of it, and shaved fourteen people on the spot.

Lille would not yield, nor Thionville, nor would the raw levies be driven from their posts in the Argonne mountains. Goethe, who, as we have said, was with the invaders, has left us a history of this campaign, from which it seems that on the 11th of October the invading army retreated from Verdun. The poet says: "It was like Pharaoh going through a red sea of mud; for here also lay broken chariots, and riders and foot seemed sinking around." His own carriage could not move, because of an unbroken column of sick-wagons which trod the town streets into a morass. The wet weather and the bad food had laid many low with dysentery and fever. At last Goethe's servant managed to shove his master's carriage into a row of wagons, and they went on, though at a funeral pace. Outside the town there was a narrow road with a ditch on the right and left. Just before him there was an ammunition wagon drawn by four horses. One horse fell, and the drivers cut the traces and let it lie. As the other three horses could not drag the ponderous machine along, they also were cut loose, and the wagon was overturned in the ditch. Goethe's carriage was driven right over the poor fallen horse, and he says, "I saw only too well how its legs, under our wheels, went crashing and quivering."

The meadows were "rained to ruin," and the foot-paths everywhere lost sight of. In the ditches and fields were dead horses enough, and sometimes they were flayed and the fleshy parts cut away, — sad tokens of the distress the army was in.

At Estain, which Goethe reached at noon, there was an endless tumult in the market-place. "All sorts of walkers, soldiers in uniform, marauders, sorrowing citizens and peasants, women and children, crushed and jostled one another amid vehicles of all sorts." While the Duke of Brunswick was thus retreating with dishonor from the task he had set himself to do, the lucky Dumouriez went to Paris to announce his success to the National Convention. He was a wiry man, of that iron cast we sometimes see, a man who was never tired, — "The creature of God and my sword," as he styled himself. He had once been foreign minister, but threw up his seal of office when Louis set his veto on the two decrees; and when Lafayette, seeing the king's cause lost, rode over the marches into Holland, the command was given to Dumouriez. He was well received in Paris, as he deserved to be, and was feasted by the citizens in grand style.

One night, however, as he was in the drawing-room of Talma, the great actor, Marat came to him unbidden and said, "I have come from the Jacobin Club to ask you why you did not pursue Brunswick with more energy."

The general turned his eyes coldly on the lean, wretched-looking Jacobin, and said with disdain, "Ah, you are he whom they call Marat!"

The very name made the company shudder; for Marat was known to be a man who had advised the murder of all the aristocrats. in France, and who would have hired assassins to butcher Talma, or Dumouriez, or any of the guests there assembled, had he thought their removal needful for the rolling on of the great Revolution to the place he had fixed in his own mind.

CHAPTER XVII.

THE TRIAL OF KING LOUIS XVI.

WE now come to a very sad and painful event in the Revolution, the trial and subsequent execution of the king. Who does not feel sorry for him? Born the heir to so much human glory, yet brought step by step to so much shame and sorrow.

There was now no king nor kingdom of France. The king was now no longer King Louis XVI., but plain Louis, or Louis Capet. The National Convention of seven hundred and forty-nine men, who first met about the middle of September, were now the sovereigns of France by might if not by right; able to raise or lower whom they would, to kill or save alive as they pleased. One of the first labors of the new Convention was to have a guard; the next was to bring to judgment those guilty of the September massacres. The guard was ordered, and then it was repealed; for it was considered an insult to Paris that a republican convention should need any protection from the people whom it so truly represented. As to the massacres, nothing was done to bring the guilty ringleaders to the gallows, though much was said and attempted. Things of greater importance than that of avenging dead men pressed upon the Convention: there was the army to quarrel over; there was the question how to feed the people of Paris; and above all, there was the question, " What is to be done with Louis?"

Much anxiety was there about the army; for the European powers were highly indignant with France for putting her king in chains, and it was thought that England would join Prussia and Austria in his defence. The French army, or armies, were in a bad way, and one member complained that thirty thousand pairs of breeches were urgently needed by the army of the South.

As for food, it was scarcer than ever, and bread riots occurred almost everywhere. Marat tells us, in his "People's Friend," that a pound of bread cost six sous, and a laborer's daily wages were but fifteen. One member proposed that every man should live two days a week on potatoes, and also that every person should hang his dog. Two of the members went one day to Chartres to arrange matters about food, and the people threatened to hang them unless they would then and there fix the price of corn to suit the pockets of the Chartres mob. And all this hunger, and these long queues of men at baker's shops, — what did they end in? The murder of the king! The queue was, as we have already said, a long line of people who stood one behind another, at the baker's door. At first there was a rope fastened to a ring in the shop wall which each person grasped with his hand; but the rope was often cut by mischief-makers, and the Convention ordered the ropes to be replaced by iron chains.

Hunger pressed on the French people still; and their overthrow of the old order of things had as yet done little or nothing to satisfy the poor with bread. People kept asking the question, "Why is food still so dear?" And the answer came, "Because Louis is still alive. We shall have no real freedom nor plenty until he is put out of the way." As long as he lived, he seemed to them a centre round which gathered plots and royalist hopes, and they thought that it should be but a short step from the Tuileries to the Place de la Révolution.

When a certain curate, Grégoire, who had become a bishop, declared from his pulpit that it was a capital crime to be a king at all, and his words were applauded as words of wisdom, we may understand what the thoughts of men were on that subject. Moreover, the eyes of Frenchmen were now suddenly turned to the pages of English history, and especially to that part of it which tells of the execution of

Charles I. Printed copies of the trial of Charles were sold in vast numbers, and the French could but reason thus: "If the English put their king to death, and have become since the first of free nations, why may not we do the same?" And so, among the questions debated in the Convention, this question, "What is to be done with the king?" became the foremost, and was the one most frequently discussed by the members.

The 6th of November was an important day for France. Her general, Dumouriez, won the battle of Jemappes, his soldiers singing, as they conquered the foe, the "Marseillaise Hymn;" and her Parliament decreed that Louis, her late king, should be brought to trial.

There was a body of members in the Convention who looked on the king's trial and what it might lead to with keen dislike. These were the Girondins. They had done much to carry on the Revolution up to this point; but now they often differed from men like Danton, Marat, and Robespierre, and many and hot were their disputes about the further progress of state affairs.

The king's trial was much affected by a discovery in the Tuileries. A certain blacksmith of Versailles, named Gamin, came one day before the Convention, and said that he had helped Louis make an iron press, which was placed in a wall of the king's chamber. He was able to point out the iron press behind some wainscot or tapestry; and the press, having been wrenched open, disclosed a number of important state letters, which brought trouble to many a man. In consequence of this the bust of Mirabeau was shattered, and several men of importance became suspected and unpopular. The blacksmith, who said the king had nearly killed him with a drugged glass of wine after the safe was securely fixed, had a large reward for his services, and the letters and papers found in the iron chest were produced as so many witnesses of the king's guilt.

On the 11th of December the king was brought in the mayor's

"IT IS A PITY TO WASTE BREAD IN TIME OF DEARTH."

carriage to the Convention hall to be tried.   The streets were full of soldiers, and the people were silent, or now and then sang snatches of the popular *Ça ira* or the " Marseillaise Hymn," as he went by. When he was in the hall, he looked around at those who were to judge him ; and the president, who had fifty-seven questions to ask him, said, " Louis, you may sit down."

After Barrère had asked his fifty-seven questions, and Louis had answered them all as well as he could, he was ordered to withdraw into a committee-room, where he partook of a crust of bread.   A clerk who was in the room having thrown some bread into the street, Louis reproved him, saying, " It is a pity to waste bread in time of dearth."

" My grandmother," observed Chaumette (a man then high in the government), " used to say to me, '.Little boy, never waste a crumb of bread, for you cannot make one.' "

" Monsieur Chaumette," replied the king, " your grandmother seems to have been a sensible woman."

Louis's trial now coming on, he was allowed to choose an advocate ; and three lawyers stepped forth to defend him ; namely, Tronchet, an old man called Malesherbes, and the youthful Desèze

It was arranged, after much debating, that Louis should again appear and plead on the day after Christmas Day.   His advocates thought it too early, but they could not get the day postponed.   So, at the cold dark hour of eight in the morning on St. Stephen's Day, the members of the Convention were at their post, and at nine o'clock Louis entered the hall to be tried, under an escort of National Guards.

The talented young Desèze did the best he could for his master. For three hours he pleaded ; and when his great effort was over, Louis fell on his neck and kissed him.   Before he left the place of trial the king also said a few words; and they were the last he ever spoke in public, except two or three on the scaffold.   He assured his judges that he was guiltless of the blood shed on the 10th of August; and then he quitted the hall, leaving his fate in the hands of those who had made themselves his judges. After many further debates it was agreed that the Convention should decide, by a majority of votes, whether Louis was or was not guilty of conspiring against liberty, and, if so, what his punishment should be. When, at length, on the 15th of January, the question was put, "Guilty or not guilty?" all voted "Aye," except twenty-eight, who did not vote at all.

The next vote was taken on the question, "What shall the punishment be?" The voting lasted from Wednesday, January 16, until the following Sunday morning. Each member had to mount, when his name was called, into the tribune, and say his say. Some voted for "death;" others for "banishment." At length "death" was decided on by a majority of fifty-three. Then came a final question, "When is he to die?" Every member had to mount the tribune again and give his vote. It was this final voting which did not come to an end until three o'clock on the Sunday morning. By a majority of seventy the question was decided, "No delay; death within twenty-four hours!"

They say that these votings formed the strangest of all the strange scenes of the Revolution. One deputy who had voted for death without delay, ran out of the hall to get some dinner in the Palais Royal; and as he was paying for it, a man stepped up to him, and said, "You voted in the king's business, did you not?"

"Yes," replied the deputy; "I voted death."

"Wretch, take that!" said the man; and the voter received a stab which caused his death in a few hours.

CHAPTER XVIII.

THE EXECUTION OF THE KING.

FROM the time that he decided to leave the Tuileries, and his brave Swiss Guard, and the gallant gentlemen who had come to fight for him, Louis became a mere puppet in the hands of the Paris municipal officers. He might have made a better fight for his crown, no doubt, but he was a quiet, peace-loving man, who shrank from bloodshed, and no doubt he did what he thought was for the best. It was a very bad best for him, though, to be cooped up, and his queenly wife as well, in a grim old tower, with thick walls and iron-grated little windows, where he could neither eat nor read nor write without some impudent fellow watching him. Was ever man so the football of a fickle fortune?

There was, however, one blessedness in his lot. His sorrows did not last long. The men who at that time ruled France soon dismissed their victims. Robespierre and Marat had this grace about them, — they were for a speedy death; and that is surely better than twenty or thirty years' imprisonment in a noisome dungeon without fire or candle. Louis had the ordinary comforts of life during his abode in the tower; but he was wounded in his spirit, day after day, by insults, which to a finely strung mind are worse than the pains of death. He was separated from his wife and children, and had but one friend to whom he could talk; and that was his valet, Cléry, who has left behind him a truthful account of his poor master's imprisonment and last hours on earth.

The Revolution was, without doubt, dead against kings and queens, and it had a delight in stripping royalty of its robes; but royalty showed itself dignified, nay, even grand, when stripped. Never did Louis appear more kinglike than in his last mournful hours.

When the Convention had decreed that he was to die so soon, the Minister of Justice was sent to the tower that Sunday about noon, or a little after, with the dreadful news. He said, when he was going, "What a frightful task for a man to have to do!"

When Louis heard that he had to die so soon, he begged hard for a respite of three days in which to prepare for his end; but they turned deaf ears to his prayer. He also asked for the consolations of religion, and this request was mercifully granted. The Abbé Edgeworth was sent to administer to his dying king all the ghostly comfort he could, and the last rites of the Church as well. The valet Cléry has given us many affecting memorials of the closing scenes in the life of his master, whom he truly loved. The king's apartments were a sitting-room and bedroom, and a small circular closet which he used as a place of prayer. It was round, from being in a round turret at a corner of the large square tower. The top was finished off outside with a roof shaped like the extinguisher of a candle. Here lived the dethroned Louis from August, 1792, until the 21st of January, 1793, when his feeble light of life was suddenly put out by the sharp edge of the axe.

On the Sunday evening, at half-past eight, he had his farewell meeting with his wife and family, who descended from the chamber above by a winding stone stair in one of the round turrets. It was a most affecting scene, — that last interview between the doomed king and his heartbroken family. It lasted an hour and three quarters, and was seen by Cléry and the officials through a glass panel in the door. They could not, however, hear a word that passed. The king was seated, with the queen on his left hand, and Madame Elizabeth, his excellent sister, on his right; the Princess Royal was in front, and

THE KING'S FAREWELL MEETING WITH HIS FAMILY.

the little Prince stood between his father's knees.   And so they (that forlorn family brought so low) spent the last Sabbath evening they were to be together in this world.   When they tore themselves asun-der, the king promised that he would see them again early on the morrow, but he did not keep his word.   When they left him that Sunday night, it was forever.

The king slept well, Cléry keeping watch in a chair, and the Abbé snatching a few hours of repose on the valet's bed.   At five o'clock Cléry lit the fire; and the noise he made aroused the king, who got up and dressed himself.   A dark January morning, cold and misty, hung over the city; but in that chilly gloom men by the hundred thousand were astir.   One great event, and only one, was in everybody's mind. The city shops were kept shut, the city streets were empty; no vehicle but one was allowed to move that morning in the highways of Paris. There was a drumming and the gathering of troops from a very early hour, and all the streets from the Temple to the Place de la Révolu-tion were lined with armed men.

In the tower itself there was a solemn service held at half-past six that morning, which was probably the most real as it was the most affect-ing of any in the borders of Christ's kingdom that day.   It was the dethroned king of France receiving his last sacrament.   A chest of drawers formed the altar on this singular occasion.   At eight o'clock the officers of justice came for him, and an hour afterward the sad procession left the tower.   The king held a book of prayers in his hand, and fixed his eyes on it as the carriage rolled slowly along the hushed streets.   The city was like a city of the dead, so silent was it then.   Every one seemed awe-struck, as well he might be, by the spectacle of a people putting its king to death.

At ten o'clock the carriage arrived at the Place de la Révolution. Did the king hope for a rescue?   Did he hope that he might hear the cry of " Vive le Roi ! " and see a solid body of his friends burst through the lines of National Guards that surrounded the guillotine?

Alas! it was not so to be. At the Temple gate some pitiful women did lift up their feeble voices on his behalf; but no man dared to cry, "God save him." If any one did feel anger or pity, he was afraid to show it; and so Louis went through a dumb city to his death, bewailed no doubt by many, but with none to strike a blow in his defence.

When he stood on the scaffold, he began a speech, in which he had just time again to avow his innocence. Fearing lest his words might produce an upstir in his favor, the officer in command ordered the drums to be beaten, and the king's voice was drowned. The officer then said, "Executioners, do your duty!" and six men seized Louis and bound him to a plank. The Abbé Edgeworth kept near, and just as the heavy axe was falling; said, "Son of Saint Louis, ascend to heaven!"

The executioner, whose name was Samson, lifted up the head, and held it out for the people to look at. Loud shouts of "Vive la République!" arose; and some of the people dipped their hand-kerchiefs, and others the points of their pikes, in the blood. "It is done! it is done!" cried the king's foes. It was indeed done, and could not be undone; but it divided the friends and it united the enemies of the Revolution.

The deputy who had been stabbed in the eating-house was buried on the Thursday after, with a great show of lamentation. The whole Convention in a body and the entire Club of the Jacobins were at the funeral.

Many who had been ardent promoters of the Revolution were horrified at the murder of the king; and especially the Girondins, who from that hour became the enemies of the more advanced men, and who, being the smaller and less popular party, were brought into the dust of death, as we shall see hereafter, though not before they had had a gallant but hopeless fight for their own principles of constitutional liberty.

CHAPTER XIX.

THE GIRONDINS.

IF you examine a map of France, you will see a department on the west coast, near the city of Bordeaux, called Gironde. A party in the French Convention who (many of them, at least) came from that district were called Girondins. This party led the Revolution for a time; but when the leaders of the mob became its leaders also, the Girondins, who were generally high-born gentlemen, saw that it would be an evil day when France was ruled by mob law. They therefore formed what we may call a Conservative party, and were hated accordingly by the rabid Republicans. The Girondins were for abolishing royalty, and yet not altogether for the murder of the king; for though many of them did vote for his death, they yet tried to get a reprieve for him, but failed in the attempt.

After the king was dead, the Girondins became yet more and more opposed to the Jacobin leaders; and at length, on May 31, 1793, the Convention was surrounded by armed multitudes, who loudly demanded the imprisonment of twenty-nine (or, as some say, thirty-three) deputies of the Girondin party. So these men, in obedience to the will of the mob, were kept under police observation; and Madame Roland, a noble Frenchwoman, the wife of the late Minister Roland, was cast into prison.

While they were thus in the strong grasp of the ruling party, Charlotte Corday stabbed Marat fatally in his bath; and this rash deed had probably much to do with the death of the Girondins generally. When Charlotte went on her errand to Paris, Barbaroux gave her a

note of introduction to the Girondin deputy Duperret; and when
Charlotte had succeeded in slaying Marat, Duperret was arrested, and
the papers were examined

At Lyons the Girondin party, who were strong, put a Jacobin
named Chalier to death. When Chalier was dying, he said that his
death would cost the city dear; and his prophecy was fulfilled.

Eleven of the Girondin deputies retreated to Bordeaux, dressed in
the uniform of National Volunteers. Every place through which they
passed bristled with dangers to them; for in each town and village
there was a Revolution Committee of a jealous temper, ever on the
look-out for men who would not go their lengths. Louvet, one of the
Girondins, has left an account of this retreat. He tells us how one of
the party was tortured with the gout, how another was too fat for
marching, and how a third had to walk on tiptoe; while Barbaroux
(the same man who had written with tears in his eyes for " six hundred
men who knew how to die'") had to limp with a sprained ankle. So
they jogged on, through perils and dangers, sleeping where they could, —
now in the summer woods, now in a straw-shed. The country got so
hot about them at last that they had to march only by night; and
once, as they passed through a mean village, they heard the dreadful words from some wakeful peasant, " There they are!" and they
glided off quickly through the darkness, over hedge and ditch, into
the wood of Quimper, and there under the wet bushes crouched together, and were found in the morning by a kind-hearted pastor, who
took them to his home and concealed them. Luckily for them, the
Quimper folk were friendly to Girondins, and allowed them to hide
themselves until a miserable little ship could be found to bear them
away to Bordeaux. There they were landed, but they found it no
place of safety. No! Tallien and the Jacobins were there with their
guillotine, cutting off the heads of all who dared to say a word against
the now powerful party in the State.

The prisons at Paris were crowded with occupants, and every day

THE GIRONDINS DISCOVERED IN THEIR HIDING-PLACE.

about the set of sun the death-carts went loaded with victims to the guillotine, which still did its dreadful work in the Place de la Révolution. The Girondins, who had been since May under the charge of the police, were now thrown into prison, and had good reason to fear the worst. Twenty-two of them, all true Republicans and all eminent men, were in course of time placed on their trial before Fouquier Tinville, the famous attorney-general.

Twenty-two Girondin members of the National Convention, who had been tried, were now to suffer death. It was the 30th of October, 1793, or, according to the new Revolutionary calendar, the 9th of Brumaire, in the year 2 of the Republic. Anno Domini was now knocked on the head, and the old months of January, February, and so on; for the Republicans, wanting everything new, constructed a brand-new almanac, which lasted fourteen years.

On the 9th of the month Brumaire, therefore, of the year 2, the twenty-two Girondins were brought to the bar of Tinville, and condemned to suffer the last dread penalty of revolution law. They were, remember, the flower of French patriots, all eloquent men, and great in their day; but now, suspected of a want of energy, they checked the glowing wheels of the great Revolution. After a lengthy trial, in which they defended themselves with surprising skill, the jury, by a fresh decree made for the purpose, declared the accused guilty, and they were sentenced to suffer the loss of life and of all their property. One of them, named Valazé, when he heard this wicked sentence, drew out a dagger and stabbed himself to the heart. The rest were taken back to prison, singing, as they went, the "Marseillaise Hymn."

Another of them, named Vergniaud, had poison with him; but he would not swallow it because he had not enough to kill his friends as well as himself. He therefore threw the poison away. The last night of the condemned Girondins was spent in a very strange manner. The fear of death does not seem to have affected their spirits in the least, for with songs and light-hearted mirth they met the " last enemy."

A vast crowd of sight-seers were out when the Girondins went forth to die. It was something new and strange, surely, to behold the Revolution thus devouring her own children; and many a man that day who saw them carted to the Place de la Révolution must have asked himself, " Who slew all these?" No rescue was attempted; and the twenty-two died, man after man, shouting, " Vive la République!" or singing the " Marseillaise Hymn " to the very last.

There they perished, those twenty-two Girondins, while some of their party who escaped had, perhaps, a still more bitter fate to encounter. Some of them were guillotined in Bordeaux. Barbaroux shot himself with a pistol; while Buzot and Pétion were found in a cornfield, their bodies half eaten by dogs. Louvet, after many dangers, happily escaped to Switzerland. Thus the Revolution began to devour her own children; and the Girondins were not the last, though they were among the best, whom she devoured.

CHAPTER XX.

CHARLOTTE CORDAY.

OUR readers will understand by this time that there were at least two parties in the State who were bitterly opposed to each other. The Jacobins, or "Men of the Mountain," were out-and-out Republicans, bent on utterly destroying all the old landmarks of society, whether rank, property, or religion; these men were the idols of the unthinking mob, and grew in power every day. The Girondins, however, wanted a republic where property, order, and religion should be respected. We have seen how the Girondins were put down, — some being thrown into prison, and some obliged to flee from Paris to get out of the reach of their stronger rivals.

A number of these men started a newspaper at Caen in opposition to the Jacobins; and the cities of Lyons, Bordeaux, and Marseilles were all minded at one time to march on Paris and put down the National Convention. Caen seems to have been a very warm centre of this anti-Jacobin spirit. Here no less than twenty-seven Girondins at one time lodged, and were entertained by those in authority; and thence they launched their "Bulletin de Caen" at the heads of Marat, Robespierre, and others.

At Caen there lived a young lady named Charlotte Corday. She was at the time she became famous about twenty-five years old, and very handsome. She had conceived a violent hatred against the cruel Marat, and she resolved to kill him if she could, though she knew very well that her own life would be sacrificed in doing the deed. She told one of the Girondins, Barbaroux by name, that she was going to Paris on some private business; and he gave her a letter to hand over to Duperret, one of the deputies in the National Convention. Charlotte set out from Caen on Tuesday, July 9, 1793, in the diligence, leaving a note for her father, in which she said that she had gone to England and he must forget her.

The diligence was full of men who talked of nothing but politics, and who were all admirers of the Jacobin side. In this conversation Charlotte took no share. On Thursday, about noon, the coach rattled over the Paris pavements; and the adventurous young lady at once ordered a room at an inn, and went to bed.

On Friday she delivered the letter to Duperret, and paid a visit to the Convention hall, for she wished to see what Marat was like. She took much notice of the " Men of the Mountain; " but Marat was not among them : he was not well, but nursing himself at home. On Saturday morning Charlotte bought a large knife wherewith to stab her victim. Having ascertained that he was living at No. 44 in the Street of the School of Medicine, she ordered a cab and was driven to the door; but when she knocked the servant came and told her that Marat was sick and could not see her. Disappointed at this, she went back to her hotel, which was called the " Inn of Providence," and sat down and wrote a letter to Citizen Marat, in which she said she could enable him to do France a signal service. To this letter no reply was sent; and she then wrote a second letter of a more pressing kind, and carried it herself to the house where Marat lived.

It was about seven o'clock in the evening of July 13 when a cab might have been seen driven along that street, and at length stopping opposite No. 44. It was the eve of a great revolutionary festival; for on the 14th, four years ago, the people of Paris stormed the Bastille. On that day Marat had distinguished himself by his conduct in the eyes of the mob, and from that day he had been growing in power. He was now, as we have said, ill, and nursing himself at home. At the very time when Charlotte Corday reached the house,

CHARLOTTE CORDAY.

Marat was having a warm bath. He was waited on by a poor woman, and he had only about twenty cents in the house. He had not, therefore, grown rich by the Revolution; and in that respect we cannot but admire the man, for no doubt he might have "feathered his nest" well by this time, had he been a covetous man.

Charlotte was determined to see Marat, and argued with the woman at the door. "I must see Citizen Marat; I can put it into his power to do France a great service." The woman was for shutting the door in Charlotte's face; but Marat, hearing her earnest voice from his slipper-bath, bade the servant admit the visitor, and she was accordingly allowed to enter the house. The sick man told her to sit down and tell him what she came about

"I am from Caen," she said, "and I have matters of importance to tell you."

"Well," said Marat, "and what are the traitors doing at Caen now? Who are there?"

Charlotte told him the names of several, — Barbaroux, Pétion, Louvet, Duchatel, and others.

"Ah, they shall be guillotined within a fortnight," exclaimed the eager Marat; and he took up his note-book, which lay on a three-legged stool close by, to write down their names. Charlotte carefully noted his actions; and as his eyes were fixed on his notebook, and his nimble fingers were writing down the names Barbaroux, Pétion, and Louvet, she drew out her bright new knife from its sheath, and drove it, with sure aim and with all the strength of her Norman right arm, deep into the heart of the "People's Friend."

He could give only one cry, "Help, my dear!" and then all was over. Marat was a dead man, and the Revolution had lost forever one of its ablest and perhaps, we may say, one of its purest leaders. For, bloody-minded as he was, he was not a selfish man; he did not overturn thrones and kill aristocrats to enrich himself, but, as he supposed and wrongly supposed, to benefit a long-suffering nation of poor, struggling laborers.

It is quite impossible to imagine, still less to describe, the rage and terror which agitated the mighty heart of Paris that Saturday evening. One weak woman had suddenly leaped into world-wide notoriety, and had made the greatest city on earth reel to and fro as if there had been an earthquake. One deputy, pale as a sheet, rushed into the Convention, shouting out, " We are all going to be murdered ! "

Paler yet lay the dead Marat; but calm and cool, her pulses beating quietly as ever, was the young woman who had treacherously and cruelly, and yet, as she believed, righteously, stabbed a man to death. The woman who came in at Marat's dying shriek ran out frantic, and alarmed every house in the street with her cries; and in a few minutes the place was crowded, and Charlotte had to defend herself from their vengeance by placing herself behind some chairs and tables, until the soldiers arrived. She was then carried away to the Abbaye Prison, to await her trial. This took place on Wednesday, July 17, and did not last long; for she said, " All these details [about the purchase of the knife, etc.] are needless. . . . It was I who stabbed Marat." And when Tinville asked her why she had done a deed so strange and terrible, she replied: " I killed him because of his crimes; I killed him to save a hundred thousand. I killed a wild beast, to give quiet to my distracted country."

As she thus confessed her guilt and declared she was alone in it, nothing more was to be said or done except to order her condemnation to death that same Wednesday evening; and about half-past seven she was led forth from her prison, habited as a murderess, in a red gown. The city, now well used to such painful sights, was more than ever crowded with people, who regarded her as she was carried to her doom with mingled feelings. Some saluted her as a martyr, by taking off their hats; and others howled at her as a devil in human shape, who had put out one of the bright lamps of the Revolution.

Beautiful, indeed, Charlotte Corday looked, on her way to the Place de la Révolution, and as calm and serene as a summer day.

She died with unfaltering courage, with a smile on her face, and " her cheeks tinged with a blush of maidenly shame," caused by the executioner's stripping her fair neck of the handkerchief which was around it.

She did the best she could for the peace of France in killing, as she thought, a wild beast; but Marat, dead in that lawless manner, was worse for France than Marat living and legislating. Nevertheless, it is a wonderful story of the energy and resolution which can sometimes find a lodging in a young woman's breast; and while there is very much in her deed to condemn, there is also something we cannot but admire.

CHAPTER XXI.

MARIE ANTOINETTE

THIS celebrated and unfortunate queen was born at Vienna in
November, 1755, being the daughter of the Emperor of Germany
and Maria Theresa of Austria. In May, 1770, she was married to
Louis the Dauphin, grandson of Louis XV. In 1774 she became
Queen of France. She was a fair young queen, and she has been described by several as she appeared in the height of her prosperity and
among all the noblest of the land. She was kindly disposed, helping
the poor, adopting orphans, and so on.

In 1777 she had a daughter, and after that a son. Her happiness
was soon overclouded; for she fell into disrepute with the French
people, and her hair grew gray with cares and sorrows. Her good
name was blackened by falsehoods, and her beauty departed from her
before its proper time. She often sat, even at Versailles, weeping in
her inner apartments, feeling that she was hated as the evil genius of
France. She had inherited, however, a strength and courage which
stood her in good stead.

During the terrible day of the insurrection of the women she alone,
they tell us, wore a face of courage, a look of lofty calmness, as if she
were one who dared to do what she felt she ought to do.

On that 6th of October, when the king had showed himself on the
balcony of Versailles to the mob, she went out too, with her boy and
girl in either hand. "No children," cried the voices; and so she
gently pushed them back, and stood there alone, with her hands
crossed on her bosom. General Lafayette took her hand, and, making

a low obeisance, kissed it; and then the people shouted, or some of them did, "Vive la Reine!" An officer, named Weber, declares that he saw one of the rough fellows levelling his musket at her, when another angrily struck it down.

Marie Antoinette's father was a Prince of Lorraine, and she ever had a drawing of her heart toward the people of that province. "Sire," said she to the king once, "these are some of your faithful Lorrainers," when some federates from that part were in Paris. She attracted the admiration of the great Mirabeau. In her he saw a courage like his own. "You do not know the queen," said he on one occasion; "her force of mind is prodigious: she is a man for courage."

Woman-like, too, was she. When it was decided to make that unfortunate flitting on the longest day of 1791, the queen must needs have a great stock of dresses made, which aroused suspicion; and she spent some five hundred louis d'ors about her toilet-case in having it arranged and forwarded, and it was lost, after all. We have already seen how she, in her broad gypsy hat, leaning on a stupid man-servant's arm, took the wrong road as they issued from the Tuileries, and, instead of going to the left hand to the glass coach that was waiting, went to the right over the Pont Royal and the river, whereby a most precious hour was wasted, and, perhaps, all was lost! We have seen, too, how the lumbering new berlin, with all the hapless royal family in it, was stopped at Varennes, and how they were all brought back with ignominy to a harsher captivity.

The queen kept up a correspondence in cipher with the emigrants and friends of the monarchy at Coblentz, but she never could persuade the duller-witted Louis to come to any decision worthy of the name. When that singular procession, called that of the Black Breeches, invaded the Tuileries, she sat with her children and their aunt behind a barricade of furniture, weeping for very shame at the ruffianism which was allowed to go on unchecked in a king's house. When a woman offered her a red cap, which she took, and placed on her little boy's fair curls, the commandant, Santerre, who brewed beer, said to her, " Madame, this people loves you more than you think."

On the yet more awful morning of the 10th of August, after a sleepless night, the queen stood with Madame Elizabeth, the king's sister, looking out of a window. " Sister," said Madame Elizabeth, " see what a beautiful sunrise ! "

When the king was entreated to leave the palace and take refuge in the Assembly, some declare that the queen said, " As for me, I would be nailed to these walls sooner; " and she then offered her husband a loaded pistol, and bade him defend his home, for now or never was his time for doing it. Others deny the truth of these things; but all admit that she behaved herself queen-like, and neither shrieked nor wept, but steeled herself to die, if she had to die, in a manner worthy of the great Theresa's daughter.

It was said by some that the queen behaved with levity while the Tuileries was sacked and burning, and while the king and she, with the Princess Lamballe, were detained in the upper story of the Assembly Hall. They say that she and her friend looked out of the window, and laughingly shook the powder from their head-dresses on the people who were walking underneath. But if this were so, it was no laughing matter soon after to be shut up in the Temple tower, and to see, as they say she saw or might have seen, the bleeding head of her dear friend the Princess Lamballe carried on a pike-point before her barred window. One municipal officer said. " Look out ; " another, of a more pitiful disposition, said, " Do not look.

During the melancholy autumn months the king was permitted, in company with his queen, to stroll in the garden of his prison at certain hours ; but the time came when this privilege was put an end to, and the afflicted pair were kept in separate apartments.

When the king had to die, in obedience to the decree of the Convention, his unhappy wife bade him farewell, as we have seen. Noth-

MARIE ANTOINETTE BEING PRERARED FOR EXECUTION.

ing is more pathetic in the range of history than that good-by. The king met his doom in January; but it was not before October that the rulers of France brought their next chief victim out of her cage, and feasted the people's eyes with her trial and execution. Those cat-eyed people are generally stealthy of foot, and awake when honester people are sleeping; and so it was that one morning at three o'clock the queen was removed to another prison. She was brought to her trial (was it not a mock one?) on the 14th of October, before the notorious Fouquier Tinville, and was arraigned as "the Widow Capet." We are glad to be told that the queen showed herself a true woman in this dreadful hour; and what better could she be?

Her accusers, of course, said what they could against her, and much more than they truthfully could; and of course, she was condemned to death. Could anything else have come of such a judge and such a jury? Impossible, when they began by assuming that it was a crime to be a queen at all. Deliver us, O Lord, from such a justice-room as that of Tinville and his creatures! Surely, the tender mercies of the wicked are cruel.

It was on Monday when the "once brightest of queens, now defaced and forsaken," stood at Tinville's bar; and one can still read in the Bulletin of the Revolutionary tribunal the "trial of the Widow Capet."

The witnesses came forward, one after another, and delivered their testimony; and the accused lady answered, when necessary, with calmness and dignity. After she was sentenced to death, which took place at four o'clock in the morning, she was asked whether she had anything to say. She replied by shaking her head. A little while after the trial was ended, the city was astir to feast its cruel eyes on the death agony of Marie Antoinette.

At sunrise the troops were drawn up, the cannon pointed in the proper direction, and every other preparation made, by the rulers of France, against any possibility of a rescue; and at eleven o'clock the queen was brought out of her dismal prison, and placed in a cart with her hands bound behind her. She was dressed in white. She had already cut off her long hair, which had become as white as snow. A priest, dressed as much like a layman as possible, went with her; but it was noticed that she spoke very little to him. Cries of "Vive la République!" arose all along the way; but the queen seemed to pay very small attention to them. When she was carried past the Tuileries, those who observed her face the most carefully saw a change in it. She was thinking of her husband and her children, and of what had been, and of what might have been had better counsels been taken. The queen reached the Place de la Révolution a little after twelve o'clock, and she mounted the scaffold with the courage of her race. The axe fell, Marie Antoinette was dead, and wild cries of "Vive la République!" arose from the infatuated mob which crowded the place.

CHAPTER XXII.

ÉGALITÉ ORLÉANS.

OUR young readers will not remember Louis Philippe, except it may be from some picture or book which they may happen to have; but he was the king of the French before the reign of the late Emperor Napoleon, and he was driven from his throne (never an easy one) by a revolution which happened in 1848. When he could no longer live safely in France, he went to England and there ended his days. He was the son of a royal duke, the Duke of Orleans, who lived during the times of the Revolution, and who, though a royal duke, was, or pretended to be, a lover of all the great changes which then took place. The name of the "Revolution Duke" was Louis Philippe Joseph. He was born in 1747, and was known, during his father's lifetime, as the Duc de Chartres. He was a handsome man, and clever, but he was not a good man. It was his bad life which made the king and queen unwilling to have him at their court, and it was their dislike of him which made him hate them, and cast in his lot with their deadly enemies. The duke had an immense fortune, — it is said he had £300,000 a year, — and this corrupted him, and made him nothing better than a mere lover of amusement. He did try to be a sailor at one time; but his courage seems to have oozed out of his fingers' ends in a battle at Ushant, when some say he hid himself in the cabin, and was laughed at as a man who did not like cannon-balls. He was very fond of driving a coach-and-four, and he loved racehorses, and gave great sums to English jockeys to mount them. But even his great income was not able to pay all he owed, and he had to sell the Palais Royal gardens to raise money for his creditors. Very early in the Revolution he showed that he was against the king, and on one occasion, when he had opposed the wish of his Majesty, he was sent away to a sort of easy kind of prison; but not for a long time. Louis was tender-hearted, and soon set his cousin at liberty; and the duke came out of bonds again, but with no kinder feelings toward his king.

When the States-General made their first procession at Versailles, it was noticed by many that the Duke of Orleans stepped before those of his own rank and tried to appear as one of the Commons, and for this feat he was rewarded with cheers; and when the Clergy and some of the Nobles joined the Commons, the duke was among them; and as soon as there was a *left* side, or party, in the Assembly favorable to the greatest changes, there the duke sat, as though he were one of them.

In the insurrection of women, when the king was insulted in his own house, and afterward brought a sort of prisoner to Paris, where was his blood relation, the Duke of Orleans? He was still making himself, by many grand promises, the idol of the people, in order that if Louis were dethroned he might be put in his place. People in England soon saw through the duke, and despised him; when they fully knew what he was up to, they shunned him as if he had the plague. A famous authoress, named Hannah More, saw him in Vauxhall Gardens, when nobody would speak to him or notice him in any way.

When the duke's money was all spent, he became the more anxious to play his cards well, so as to climb into power; and he thought he could not do better than sit among the thirty members on the left, and go as far in the Revolution as any of them. But it was plainly to be seen what he was after. When the debates were going on about the regency, he was observed anxiously walking up and down the passages of the Parliament House; but his hopes were doomed to be crushed, and no man pitied him, for he was loved by none. When he was disappointed, he seemed disposed to be sorry for the king's misfortunes; and one Sunday he went to a court levee, having sent word beforehand that he was far from being the king's enemy, as it was commonly said of him. At this levee, however, the duke was shamefully treated, for the courtiers flocked round him and elbowed him to the door; and when he retired to another room, where a table was laid with silver dishes and such-like, voices were heard saying, "Take care of the plate!" as if the duke were a common burglar. On that occasion he never got within sight or speaking range of the royal family; and when he was fairly driven down the staircase to the outer door, some of the courtly group actually spat on his head. All this ungentlemanly treatment was unknown to the king at the time, and when he heard about it afterward he was greatly offended. But the Duke of Orleans attributed it to him, and he hated him from that day forth with a deeper hatred than ever.

When the National Convention was chosen, the duke was one of the sixty members of the former Parliament who were elected. As now all ranks and titles were swept away, the duke was no longer a duke, and he therefore asked his Paris electors to give him a new name worthy of the glorious age they lived in. One of them therefore suggested the name Égalité, — that is, Equality, — and the duke thenceforth sat among his friends as Philippe Égalité. But in spite of all his loud professions, and all he had given up for the Republic, Philippe Égalité was never trusted by the stern men with whom he sat and voted. These men always suspected him as a dangerous "mingle-mangle" of royalty and republic. His face, they say, grew more and more gloomy, as though he knew he were treading on a very uncertain path, which might lead him any day to the guillotine.

When the great hour came for deciding how the king was to be dealt with, and some were for banishment and some for death, Philippe mounted the tribune and spoke his word of fate thus: "In my soul and conscience I vote for death." At the sound of his voice a groan and a shudder ran through the hall. Philippe hit his mark; he helped to slay his kinsman, but in killing him he destroyed himself. When the other vote had to be taken, "Shall there be delay or not in the king's death?" here again the unnatural kinsman voted, "No delay!" and the next one who voted, to show his disgust, said, as he mounted the tribune, "Since Philippe says no, I, for my part, say yes."

When Louis was put to death on Monday, January 21, in the Place de la Révolution, Philippe Égalité was near the scaffold. He sat in his cabriolet by the guillotine, and when the last act in that sad drama was over the wretched duke drove away. On the 6th of April that same year, as he was sitting at the whist-table in his palace, he was "wanted" by the Convention. One of their bailiffs came for him, and he was obliged to go. He was examined, and found guilty of crimes against the Revolution; and he was sent to the Castle of If, near Marseilles; and his "Palace Égalité,' once known as the Palais Royal, became the Palais National.

Nearly seven months afterward he was brought to Paris, and found guilty of "Royalism" and other crimes. In the mind of many he was guilty because he had voted in his soul and conscience for the king's death. On the 3d of November he reached Paris, and on the 6th he was doomed to die at once. After he heard the sentence he partook of a very good breakfast, and then awaited his terrible fate with great coolness. He was carried to the place of execution, dressed with uncommon elegance; but he found none to pity him in all that great crowd through which he went. Every mouth, rather, was opened to pour out its cursing and bitterness; and as he went by his once elegant home, the people took hold of the horses' heads, and made the death-cart stop awhile, that the duke might see it and be pained by its changed appearance. There, in great letters (each blue, white, and red), he could read these words: "Republic, one and

THE DUKE OF ORLEANS GOING TO EXECUTION.

indivisible; Liberty, Equality, Fraternity, or Death. This is National Property."

Looking on his old home thus given up to the people whom he hated, Égalité died; and with much coolness and unconcern, for he was a brave man, and might, perhaps, have been a great one had he been differently placed. But by foolishly and wickedly pandering to a furious mob, he earned (as all who do so will) their deadly contempt; and they were right so far in despising him, for he was a double-faced man, — and as such, a man to be despised, though not to be visited with the extreme penalty of the law.

CHAPTER XXIII.

THE OVERTHROW OF RELIGION.

HOW did the Christian religion fare in all these unquiet times? It fared very badly, — that is, the outer show of it; for, it must be confessed, the ministers of religion were, when the Revolution began, not what they should have been. Had they been so, the Revolution would never have taken place at all.

It was thought by many good Republicans that the French Revolution was really a great effort to realize the Christian religion. Its three watchwords, Liberty, Equality, and Fraternity, look very fair and sweet to the eye ; and no doubt many simple-minded Frenchmen, who were disgusted with the hollow shell of Christianity which was offered them as the highest possible form of religion, did hope that the Revolution would bring not only plenty of bread, but a pure faith also. But, alas for their hopes! how sorely they were disappointed! On every burial-ground it was ordained that these words should be inscribed · " Here is eternal sleep."

No; the temper of the French people was not favorable to the old forms and practices of religion, and in the month of November, 1793, the "Feast of Reason" was appointed in the place of the old Christian feasts of Easter and Christmas. There was to be henceforth no religion but liberty, and the only God to be worshipped was " The People."

Then began the curious and painful scenes of churches losing their bells, which were cast into the melting-pots to come out fused metal for the moulds of cannon; and those old melodious bells, made in

happier times to chime their sweetest on holy days, and to call people
to the mercy-seat of Our Father, were now forced to assume a new
shape, and send forth volleys of deadly missiles. The sacred cups and
patens, if of silver, were trundled away to the Mint to become pieces of
money; and where the church had only pewter vessels, they were
melted and cast into bullets to slay the enemies of France.

The vestries, once full of richly embroidered garments, were left
naked and empty. Surplices became shirts, and costly copes were
transformed into coats or trousers. The service-books were made
into wadding for muskets, and even the graves were broken open
for the sake of the lead of which the coffins were made.

The sepulchre of a long line of kings was called St. Denis. This
name was not pleasing to the men in power, and it was changed into
the name of " Franciade." What cared a red-capped Republican for
St. Denis?

So in the winter months of 1793 one might see strange sights
in Paris and in other French cities, — drunken men riding on asses,
a chalice full of brandy in one hand and a paten with some tid-bit on
it in the other. The ass, perhaps, would have, as a bit in his jaws,
the black or colored silk stole of a priest. A long line of such un-
seemly rioters, with an immense quantity of church furniture carried
on the backs of asses and in wheelbarrows, went to the hall of the Convention, and stood there to receive an ovation, as if they had been engaged in the most praiseworthy work possible. Some witty fellow had
written a suitable poem, which was sung; and the chorus was joined in
by drunken revellers, who brandished cross and crucifix and swung
censers about. Some of the members, Danton especially, were very
angry at this wicked spectacle, which was indeed enough to bring the
Convention into contempt in the judgment of mankind; but the greater
part of those foolish law-makers seem to have applauded these goings on,
and to have permitted the drunken ruffians to dance the carmagnole in
the hall; nay, some of the more advanced Republicans, rejoicing in the

complete overthrow of the Christian religion (in their eyes a mere sham), came out of their seats and danced with the girls, many of whom were attired in priests' vestments. To such a pass had the French come in the November of 1793. But when we remember how the old cathedrals in England were treated by the rude soldiers of Oliver Cromwell, we shall be more slow to condemn the French, who were for a time drunk with the new wine of their liberty, and hardly knew what they were doing. The English soldiers were trained, indeed, to hate with a deadly hatred all the "rags of popery," as they called the decent ornaments of the clergy, and the sweet-voiced organs, and the church ornaments, and painted windows; but they never dethroned God, nor set up a miserable opera-singer in his place as the French did. To such a fool's pass did those miserable men come under the guiding hand of a wretched creature who went by the loudly sounding name of Anaxagoras Chaumette. This man had been a sailor in his youthful days, and he was now a great man, or thought so. Anyhow he was a ready speaker, and he had plenty of boldness and a fair supply of wit; but his long curly hair covered a rather vain and empty head.

It was Chaumette who conceived the brilliant notion of a Feast of Reason, and a goddess to match it. A goddess, — yes, none less than a dancer at the opera, named Candeille, who, when well painted and dressed in sky blue, with a garland of oak leaves on her head, was carried first into the hall of the Convention, and afterward into the Cathedral of Our Lady, when she was seated (where does the reader imagine?) on the high altar itself!

This theatre goddess was accompanied to the cathedral by many grave and reverend senators, a number of select citizens dressed as Romans, bands of music, and a vast multitude wearing the red night-cap; and a hymn to Liberty, having been written by a poet, was duly sung. Anaxagoras Chaumette must have felt himself a great man that day; for he had made a religion, and a goddess to boot. It was a

THE OVERTHROW OF RELIGION.

grand stroke of business for that curly-headed sailor; but we cannot help thinking he would have been happier and more useful had he stuck to his ship, and left gods and goddesses alone. When he brought the ský-blue dancer into the aisle of Notre Dame, how little he thought he would soon have to meet the God whom he had insulted!

We will not dwell any longer on these painful pictures of blasphemy, profanity, and robbery, which were seen in all parts of France, until almost every house of prayer was stripped and desolate, and the people were left without a religion except those dry bones of a miserable sham called the Feast of Reason. This was the poor man's festival, and an opera-dancer was his deity! Verily, the Revolution was not lucky in its religion; that, at least, must be admitted by every candid mind.

11

CHAPTER XXIV

ARREST OF DANTON.

WE have seen the Girondins, those true children of the Revolution, thrust out of the Convention, and then put under arrest; we have seen some of them flying disguised over France, and others, who could not escape, brought before the judgment-seat of Fouquier Tinville, and sentenced to a speedy death. It is strange to think that Barbaroux, the handsome and eloquent Republican, who sent for the six hundred Marseillese, had at last to shoot himself to avoid falling, as he feared, into the hands of the pitiless Jacobins. It is also strange to think that Pétion, once the almost adored Mayor of Paris, should have to fly from the more advanced Republicans, and should die in a cornfield and be found half eaten by dogs. But so it was. The Girondins helped to raise a spirit which neither they nor any one else could control. They gave life to a power which turned upon them and rent them in pieces. As one of them said: " The Revolution, like Saturn, devoured its own children."

But the devouring appetite of the Revolution did not stop at the Girondins. Far from it. The Committee of Public Safety, formed of nine leading members, was soon supreme; and as it had men in it like Robespierre and the cruel Billaud (who looked on with satisfaction at the September massacres), we are not surprised to see men dragged down to the axe who ought to have been safe enough, — men such as Danton and Camille Desmoulins, who had, more than any others, helped on the Revolution from the very first. It was Danton himself who proposed that all power should be given to the Committee of

Public Safety, and that it should have a very large sum of money at its command. But Danton would not sit in the Committee himself, though they requested him to do so many times. He grumbled loudly at the shameful way the people went on in the churches, for he felt it would bring the Revolution into discredit, as no doubt it did. Other things, too, did not please Danton. He saw that the members of the Convention were becoming afraid, many of them at least, to speak their minds. One of them, named Chabot, talked of forming an opposition, and in another week he was in prison. For any member could get on his legs and propose the impeachment of any other member; and if the proposition was carried, the accused member was swiftly arrested, brought before Tinville and his jurymen, and carted off to the guillotine. It was a fearful time, especially for those who meddled with government; and it was well called the "Reign of Terror," for nobody seems to have known whether or not his head would remain on his shoulders from one week's end to another.

The generals, too, of the Revolutionary armies had no very pleasant time of it. If a general did not win a victory, he was sent for, and had to stand a searching examination. One general, named Houchard, was guillotined because he stood behind a hedge during a battle. Every officer felt that he must go forward and storm the enemy's position; for if he did not do his best, and more than his best, he knew he would have to lose his head at Paris. It was now that several famous men started up from the ranks and led French armies to victory. We may mention Jourdan, Pichegru, and Hoche, among others. There were not less than fourteen armies who kept the numerous enemies at bay; and those armies were made up of clever French lads, who were soon drilled into the finest soldiers ever seen. France has never shown herself greater or so great as when at this time she rose up, one nation against many, and hurled back her enemies on every side. That, at least, was a sublime sight; and however much we may mourn over the sorrow and terror caused by the Revolution, we cannot help admiring the dauntless bravery of those boys who, often without shoes and almost always in rags, swept away the pipe-clayed soldiers of Prussia with their shouts of *Ça ira!*

We might fill page after page with the horrors which were perpetrated in the unhappy country districts of France. We might tell our readers more about the headsman at Nantes, who was worn out with guillotine work; of ninety priests sunk at one time in a flat-bottomed boat in the Loire; of women and children, by the five hundred, shot down in La Vendée; of men and women tied together and flung into the river, which tying together was called in jest a " republican marriage." It was a fine time for the ravens and wolves: they had many a feast on human flesh. Mothers had sometimes to stand by the guillotine and see their children executed, and the innocents were often thrown into the cold, dark river after their mothers; and when the murderers were asked to spare the little ones, they answered, " These children are wolflings, who will grow, if they live, to be wolves."

The Committee of Public Safety consisted, as we have said, of nine, members; and, by Danton's decree, it was made all powerful, — yea, powerful enough to drag him down, though he was the giant of the Revolution.

On the 15th of March, 1794, a batch of the most advanced men were suddenly arrested and brought to trial. Among them was the church-robber Chaumette, and others whom the stronger party suspected. Every one was now suspected in turn, and it was a question, Who could eat the other? Danton was not a bloodthirsty man like some of them, nor a selfish man. He had often been heard to say, " Let Danton's name be blighted, so long as France is free." And he had also said, when he saw the quarrels and disputes among the Revolutionary leaders, " Peace! oh, peace with one another! Are we not alone against the world, — a little band of brothers?"

In the same March Danton left Paris for a few days. He was, perhaps, unwise to do so. He visited his birthplace, Arcis-on-the-

"DANTON, NO WEAKNESS!"

Aube, and enjoyed, as far as he could, a few peaceful days; but he was soon sent for, and had to return from the sweet murmur of the stream and the fresh green fields to measure his strength with Robespierre, and to fail in the attempt.

When he returned to his place in the Convention, he said, "We ought to put down the Royalists, but we should not confound the innocent with the guilty."

"And who told you," said Robespierre, "that one innocent person ever has perished?"

"Not one innocent person?" replied Danton; "what do you say, friend Paris?" Here he turned to a man who, as a juryman, had had much to do with the trials and condemnations. What friend Paris answered we do not know, but he must have felt qualms of conscience.

Danton was advised to get into the Tribune, and crush Robespierre, as he easily might have done. He was warned that if he did not put down that man, that man would put him down. But he was not of a suspicious temper, and he thought, as he had done so very much for the Revolution, his life would be safe. When his friends advised him to fly, he said he would not. "If I am cast out from France," said he, "there is nothing for me in other lands but a prison. I would rather stay where I am." Even on the night of March 30, when his friend Paris came in and told him that his arrest had been made out in the Committee of Public Safety, he would not stir. "They dare not arrest me," he said; and he went to bed as if nothing had happened.

Early next morning it was rumored over Paris that Danton and several others had been arrested. "Who, then," asked every one, "is safe?" Danton, when he heard it, said that he had a year ago created that same Committee of Public Safety, and had armed it with supreme power; but he now saw his mistake, and asked God and man to pardon him for what he had done. "They are all brothers Cain," said he, "and not one of them understands anything about government."

When he was brought before Tinville, and asked what was his name he answered, " My name is Danton, a name tolerably well known in the Revolution; and my abode will soon be annihilation." The trial of Danton was the hardest task Tinville had ever had, and unless the Committee of Public Safety had passed a new decree he would never have been condemned; but the decree was passed, and Danton, by law, was condemned to die. He died, as he had lived, a true *man !* His courage was nearly giving way, as he thought of his dear wife left weeping behind; but he soon remembered who he was, and he encouraged himself to die bravely, by saying, " Danton, no weakness! "

Just before he died he said to Samson the executioner, " Show my head to the people; it is worth showing." With him died several other leading men, including Camille Desmoulins, the editor; and we can but say here, as we said once before, that the Revolution was now, like Saturn, eating her own children.

CHAPTER XXV

THE FALL OF ROBESPIERRE.

MAXIMILIEN ROBESPIERRE has left behind him a name which is as detestable as any in history. " He was a man," said Condorcet, " without an idea in his head or a feeling in his heart." And yet he rose to be the first man, for a time, in France. He was the son of an advocate at Arras, and a school-fellow with the brilliant Camille Desmoulins. When he became a member of the States-General, he was about thirty years of age ; he wore spectacles, and his complexion was of a bilious hue. He soon attracted the notice of Mirabeau, who thought " he would do something, because he believed every word he spoke."

When the Jacobin Club used to meet in its early days, Robespierre was always present; and when there were but thirty members seated on the extreme left in the National Assembly, he was one of them, and not ashamed of his opinions. In 1791 he was elected Public Accuser in the new courts of justice. Brave he never was, for he used to disappear at the times when there was a crisis, such as that of the 9th of August, 1792. When the belfries were sounding at midnight, and all the people were getting ready, and the six hundred Marseillese were leading the way to the Tuileries, Robespierre hid himself, and he did not come out of his den until the king was put under lock and key, and so rendered powerless.

But this want of pluck does not seem to have lessened Robespierre's influence with the Jacobins. That powerful club met in the nave of the Jacobins' Church, which was seated up to the very roof.

The tribune, where the speakers stood when speaking, was raised about half-way between the pavement and the roof. The chief speaker in this remarkable assemblage was Robespierre; he was the Jacobins' petted child, and they would listen, hour after hour, to his long-winded orations.

When the September massacres were over, and a thousand and eighty-nine lay dead, and the carters carted the stripped human bodies away at so much per journey to the burying-grounds, Robespierre nearly wept when he heard it said that there was one innocent person among the slain. The Girondins, who saw the dangerous principles of Marat and Robespierre, rose up and denounced them; and both were in some peril, but escaped it.

One day Robespierre was in the tribune and said, "Is there any one here that dare accuse me of aspiring to be a dictator?"

"Yes," replied Louvet, starting up and taking some papers from his pocket; "I accuse thee, Robespierre, — I, Jean Baptiste Louvet."

"Speak, Robespierre!" shouted Danton; "speak in thine own defence."

But the accused, turning pale, did not answer a word. And Louvet went on with his papers, reciting one crime after another, — how he bullied at elections, had a retinue of mob soldiers, wished to be a dictator, had his hands stained with the blood of innocent victims in the September massacres, and so on.

The whole Convention was in an uproar, and never, it is said, did Robespierre stand in such peril; but the Convention, eager for public matters, dismissed the affair as a mere personal quarrel between Robespierre and Louvet.

In the great trial of the king, Robespierre, of course, both spoke and voted for his death. When the French lawyers were endeavoring to prove the trial lawful, Robespierre said, "What is the use of talking about the law? Here might is right."

Danton, as we have seen, had moved that all power should be given to the Committee of Public Safety, though he afterward asked pardon of God and man for thus putting such a fearful weapon into the hands of nine men who were " all brothers Cain."

Robespierre was, of course, one of those nine ; and he hoped by means of his own adroitness to remove all his rivals from his path, and to become by and by a sort of French Cromwell. His wishes had become a law by the end of 1793, and he now conceived himself strong enough to pluck down Danton, the only one of whom he was afraid.

About the beginning of April, 1794, the great Danton and several of his supporters were put to death. Among them was the brilliant writer Camille Desmoulins, a bosom friend of Danton. These two died in the prime of life, one being thirty-four, and the other a year older. Camille's widow followed him on the 10th of April, and many others. Terrible now was Robespierre, the leading spirit of the Committee of Public Safety; and many were the heads which now fell into the sack. Among them we may notice that of the once honored Madame Elizabeth, the sister of Louis. Only two members of the royal family now remained, — a boy and a girl. The unfortunate boy was taken away from Marie Antoinette while she was alive, and handed over to the tender mercies of a cordwainer, named Simon, who taught the lad to be as rough as himself.

When Simon became a member of the Municipal Council, the boy hid himself in the Temple Prison and was utterly neglected. He very nearly perished of hunger, and had to wear his shirt for six months without washing or changing it.

Robespierre was anxious to have some sort of religion for the Republic ; and as the old faith was destroyed and the worship of Reason set on one side, he invented a religion, with the help of his friends, for poor France. On a bright June day, in 1794, the Tuileries garden was crowded with people in their best clothes, and Robespierre, having made the Convention pass some decrees about a

Supreme Being and the immortality of the soul, came forth at their head, dressed in a sky-blue coat, white waistcoat embroidered with silver, and black silk breeches. David, the painter, had prepared some hideous pasteboard figures of Atheism and Anarchy ; and when Robespierre had made a speech, the painter handed him a lighted torch, wherewith he set fire to the figures and burned them to ashes. Then there arose by aid of machinery a statue of Wisdom, which got rather scorched by the flame.

It seems that Robespierre was rather laughed at by the shrewd French people for the part he had taken in this silly affair, and he was sulky for some time afterward. There was a statesman named Tallien, who had been suspected, and recalled from Bordeaux. At this man Robespierre had launched threats from the tribune. There were many others, also, who believed that they were soon to be marked out for slaughter. It was said that there were forty, at least, who were to be struck down at a blow, and then Robespierre was to be made a dictator, and be in reality the sovereign of France.

At a dinner-party near Paris, on a very hot day in July, the guests took off their coats, and left them in the drawing-room. One of them, named Carnot, requiring some paper, groped in Robespierre's pocket, and found a list of forty names, his own being among them. Of course he did not go back to the company, but made his way at once into a place of safety.

On the 26th of July Robespierre mounted the tribune, and spoke of the bad state of Republican spirit, and of the need of new vigor to be given to the guillotine. The speech fell flat, and the usually obsequious Convention was mutinous. He felt that the hour was now come when either he must put the Convention down, or it must put him down. He went that same night to the Jacobins, and told them how he had been treated ; and they shouted out that their Robespierre should not die, but there should be another insurrection, and the Convention should be cleared of all who did not obey Robespierre.

ROBESPIERRE TRYING TO KILL HIMSELF.

On the morrow, as Saint Just, one of Robespierre's creatures, was reading a report, Tallien entered and interrupted him. He said, " If this Convention dares not strike the tyrant, I will; and with this will I do it!" At these words he drew out a dagger.

Then ensued a fearful scene. Robespierre tried again and again to speak, but he could not get a hearing for the noise. He turned and appealed to each party, but none would pay the least attention now to his words.

" The blood of Danton chokes him," they said.

He was decreed accused, and his brother also, and Saint Just, and other friends of his; and they were packed off to prison. But they were rescued by some National Guards whom Henriot the commander had corrupted, and things looked very doubtful for some time. The Convention, however, declared them outlaws, and made Barras general of such troops as they could get together.

There was nearly a battle between Henriot's men and those of Barras, and there would have been, had not the Convention's decree been read aloud : " Robespierre and all rebels are declared out of law." Then the soldiers all forsook Henriot, and joined Barras.

The wretched Robespierre and his company were now come to their death, and they knew it. Henriot flung himself out of the window, and lodged in a cesspool, whence he was taken out half dead. Augustine Robespierre followed Henriot; Couthon tried to kill himself; Saint Just called on Lebas to kill him; Robespierre tried to blow out his brains, but failed, breaking his lower jaw instead. They were all tried, and condemned to death, and were guillotined that same afternoon in the Place de la Révolution; and with their execution what was called the Reign of Terror came to an end.

CHAPTER XXVI.

THE DAY OF THE SECTIONS.

SUCH is the name given to the 5th of October, 1795, the last day of the Revolution, and the first day of Napoleon's real power. Robespierre fell, as we have seen, in July, 1794, and after his fall every one seemed to breathe more easily. The word "mercy" was once more heard in France. The Convention became supreme again, and free discussion went on, and the prisons were opened, and the suspects set free; the Jacobin club-room was locked up, and its key laid on the table of the Convention; the key was given up again, but the glory of the Jacobins was over. The moderate men rose in favor every day. Paris became again a joyous city, a city of song and dance; and the ruffianism of St. Antoine was kept in check by young fellows of the respectable classes, who formed themselves into well-drilled bands, and carried clubs loaded with lead. They used to say, "We have suffered enough, our friends have been guillotined: down with these cursed Jacobins!"— or, sometimes, "Jacoquins" (*coquin* being the word for "rascal"). On the 29th of November, 1794, these armed dandies of Paris attacked the Jacobin club-room, and smashed the windows. This led to a scrimmage outside, where the Jacobin members had the worst of it, and the troops were obliged to interfere, after which this once mighty club was finally closed as a nuisance.

But the Paris mob looked upon all these revivals of genteel life with the greatest dislike. The bakers' *queues* were still as long as ever they were, bread was very dear, trade was slack, and on the 1st of April, 1795, St. Antoine rose again, and flowed in a solid mass

toward the Tuileries, shouting out, " Bread! bread!" The Convention
was sitting when the great sea of people flowed like an irresistible tide
into the hall; but, the alarm having been sounded, they were swept
out again by some National Guards, assisted by the young volunteer
gentry, who did not use their clubs loaded with lead, but actual
bayonets.

In this year Fouquier Tinville, who had sent so many to a bloody
death, was himself guillotined, and sixteen of his jurymen with him.
They all pleaded hard for their lives, saying they had acted by order
of the Committee of Public Safety. At Lyons great conflicts went
on between the moderate men and the Jacobins. Sixty of the latter
were burned to death, or stifled by smoke; and the Jacobins in other
places avenged their Lyons brethren by killing or maiming those who
were opposed to them.

At Paris, too, the old cry was again raised among the leaders of the
mob, " To arms! to arms!" and the old scenes were enacted. Crowds
armed with pikes and muskets filled the galleries and hall of the
National Convention. Women were there, by the thousand, clamoring for bread; and the husbands, hearing that the Convention was
assassinating their wives and daughters, burst open the doors and
seized hold of Deputy Ferand, who was endeavoring to shield the
President from injury. They trampled him under their feet, and
dragged him nearly dead into the lobby, and then beheaded him; and
once more this wild city saw its favorite sight of a bleeding head and
a deathly face uplifted on a pike's point, and making the circuit of
the principal streets. The bulk of the mob still remained in the
Convention hall, its leaders insisting on this and that decree being
passed at once; but the President, Boissy d'Anglas, would not yield,—
no, not for a moment, though the wretches levelled muskets at him,
and shook Feraud's gory head in his face. It was a frightful din,—
men shouting, drums beaten, honorable members escaping when they
could; no order, no law possible.

. At four o'clock about sixty members were left; and they, in obedience to mob law, chose a president (for the real President had left the hall), and passed a number of decrees of a highly revolutionary character. While the people were thus triumphing over their success, and shouting out, "Decreed! decreed!" with a roll of drum music, an officer entered, followed by a number of National Guards and young gentlemen with fixed bayonets. These, with measured tramp, very soon cleared the place, many of the mob throwing open the windows and escaping that way. All the decrees that had been passed were declared null and void; and thirteen of the sixty who had passed them were accused, but not at once arrested. They, in a day or two afterward, set up a new National Convention in the east of Paris, and also a rival force; but the dashing sparks of Paris gentry proved too much for St. Antoine, and they cowed that noisy suburb and disarmed it. The actual murderer of Feraud was captured and all but guillotined. He was rescued by the men of St. Antoine, and he hid himself in one of the courts of this populous suburb; but hearing that St. Antoine was beaten and to be disarmed, he threw himself headlong from a lofty roof, and died miserably

Of the thirteen members who passed the decrees, all perished by the guillotine except three. Ruhl shot himself through the head; and Goujon, when he heard that he was sentenced, drew a knife, sheathed it in his breast, then handed it on to Romme, who did the same, and then quickly passed it to the next, who all but slew himself.

The 5th of October in that year was a day of very great importance to Europe, for it raised Napoleon Bonaparte out of obscurity into fame. That day saw him starting on his wonderful path of glory, and it also brought a certain amount of peace and order to the long-distracted city, though it was order brought about by the great soldier's sword.

The Convention, wishing to end its labors, presented to the country a constitution. Many of its provisions irritated the Paris

HOLDING UP THE HEAD OF FERAUD ON A PIKE.

Sections, who, sooner than accept it, massed their forty thousand fighting men to resist it. The Convention had also its regular troops, but not nearly so many; and it had its officers, with Menou at the head. On the 4th of October the Convention ordered Menou to go and disarm the rebels; he went, but returned without any success, and was thrown into prison as a traitor. The rebels were emboldened at Menou's ignominious failure, and the Convention was disheartened. What were they to do? Some thought Barras was the man to disarm the rebels. Others, more to the purpose, bethought them of Bonaparte. The command was offered to him, and in half an hour it was accepted. And then the readiness and military talent of Bonaparte showed themselves. He at once sent off Murat at a gallop to secure the guns at the camp of Sablons. Murat arrived just in time to prevent them from falling into the other party's hands. Then the young general Napoleon made all his arrangements as only he could make them. " He drew a ring of steel discipline round the Tuileries, and saw that every gunner had his match burning," and that every soldier was on the alert. The 5th of October came, the anniversary of the insurrection of women, and the rebels of the Sections were counting on an easy victory over the Convention, and of making it bend to their wishes.

The rebels seized the Church of St. Roch, and the Pont Neuf. The outposts of the Convention fell back, and every now and then a stray bullet struck the Tuileries. There was a wish on the part of the Sectioners to settle the matter without bloodshed, and many women were busy as peacemakers; but Napoleon had his orders to repel the rebels by force, and he was not a man to shrink from the task.

Four o'clock in the afternoon arrived, and the rebels, finding no response to their messages of peace, began the attack on the Convention in earnest, upon which General Bonaparte ordered his great guns to be fired. In a few minutes two hundred of the rebels were blown to pieces, especially near the Church of St. Roch; and the Section soldiers, finding themselves exposed to such terrible discharges of grape, retired in all directions, and after a few more shells had been fired the whole affair was over.   The Church of St. Roch shows to this day the marks of the cannon-balls.   The Citizen Bonaparte, who had thus caused the Convention to triumph, was named by acclamation General of the Interior; and Paris felt at last that she had met her match in him who may with truth be called the First Soldier of his own time.

THE END.